Fashion Inspires

Married to the

Fashion

The

Muse

Cinematic Muse

The

The Princess Brides

The American Muse

Muse of the

Moment

Fashion Muse

The Inspiration Behind Iconic Design

Fashion Muse

Muse

The Inspiration
Behind Iconic Design

Debra N. Mancoff

PRESTEL

Munich · London · New York

Contents

The Cinematic Muse

Mannequins, Models, and the Muse

Shock Value

History and Heritage

The American Muse

The Princess Brides

Introduction: A Special Love Affair

Hubert de Givenchy was hard at work on his 1954 Spring/Summer collection when an assistant announced an unexpected visitor. Although the young designer disliked interruptions, he was more than willing to receive "Miss Hepburn." As head of his own salon for just two years, Givenchy had earned a reputation for superbly crafted, feminine designs, and he already counted a number of film stars among his valued clientele. "Miss Hepburn" was one of his favorites, so he put aside his work and went to greet her. But rather than the famous actress, he encountered a slender, winsome, wide-eyed woman dressed in slim pants and flats. It was not the stately Katherine Hepburn but the sprightly Audrey Hepburn, an as-yet-unknown actress, looking to find a few special garments to wear in an upcoming film. Givenchy's surprise quickly transformed into delight. He was captivated by Hepburn's delicate beauty and exquisite manners, but he was pressed for time. So instead of creating the garments that she required, he allowed her to make a selection from a previous collection. She chose wisely—the gowns she wore by Givenchy in the film *Sabrina* were unforgettable—but their instant rapport was far more significant. They began a life-long friendship that Givenchy describes as "a special love affair." In Givenchy, Hepburn discovered a kindred artistic spirit, and in Hepburn, Givenchy discovered his muse.

The concept of the muse—the incarnation of creative inspiration—has origins in ancient Greek mythology. As told by the poet Hesiod in the *Theogony* (ca. 700 BCE), Zeus, the head of the Olympian gods, developed a passion for

Mnemosyne, the goddess of memory. For nine sequential nights, he visited her chambers, and nine months later she gave birth to nine daughters. The daughters made their home at the foot of Mount Olympus, where they would dance and sing for the pleasure of their father. And in their songs, they celebrated the divine powers of the gods and the heroic deeds of men. Hesiod named them— Calliope, Clio, Erato, Euterpe, Melpomene, Polyhymnia, Terpsichore, Thalia, and Urania—and declared that they inspired his poetry by teaching him the value of turning wisdom into song so that future generations would not forget the past. He called them the Muses, from the Greek word *mousai*, or mountain, in honor of their dwelling in the foothills of Mount Olympus. To spark the flame of inspiration, poets would begin their compositions with an invocation to the Muses.

Over the centuries, the formulation of the Muses expanded and evolved. Each Muse became connected with a specific endeavor: Clio with history; Terpsichore with dance; Euterpe with music. They acquired attributes that signaled their individual identities: a scroll, a lyre, a flute. At the same time, the term *muse* came to indicate the presiding spirit behind all artistic inspiration—visual as well as literary—and that idea was most often represented in the form of a beautiful woman. In the painting *Pastoral Concert* (1510), Titian portrays two young men, singing to the music of a lute. They are in the company of two female figures, whose nudity and symbolic gestures reveal that they are not mortal women, but personifications, representing the very

Giulio Romano, *Apollo Dancing with Muses*, 1540, Galleria Palatina, Palazzo Pitti, Florence

Following double page: Audrey Hepburn in a scene from the film *Breakfast at Tiffany's*, New York, 1960

essence of creativity. The figure on the right holds a flute, a sign that she is one of Mnemosyne's daughters, Euterpe, the Muse of music. But the figure on the left is not one of the Nine Muses. Her attribute, the pitcher with which she replenishes the well, indicates that she is an embodiment of inspiration—the wellspring of creative activity—and her presence serves as a catalyst to ignite artistic endeavor.

It is easy to understand that a fashion designer would similarly conceive inspiration in human form, and many designers have sought and found their own muse in a beautiful woman. But few associations have been as richly rewarding and enduring as that of Hubert de Givenchy and Audrey Hepburn. Both recalled separately—and repeatedly—that their connection was instantaneous. To Hepburn, Givenchy was more than a designer; he helped her project the indelible image that changed the face of American beauty. Dressed in his designs, she created the "Audrey Look," youthful with a sophisticated polish, mannerly with a touch of mischief, exquisite but always approachable. He became her favorite designer both onscreen and off, and through the decades he also became her dearest, most trusted friend. For Givenchy, Hepburn was more than the ideal client; with her slender figure, delicate beauty, and playful spirit, she was the very embodiment of his aesthetic. Her wardrobe selections for the film *Sabrina* (1954)—it had been her idea to approach Givenchy—won him the Oscar in 1955 for costume design from the American Academy of Motion Picture Arts and Sciences. Over the years his designs for her

film characters reached iconic status: the collection for the "Quality" woman in *Funny
Face* (1957), the little black dresses in *Breakfast at Tiffany's* (1961), the ladylike
coats and matching hats in jewel-toned woolens for *Charade* (1963). In each case,
he was designing for a character in a film script, but his ultimate inspiration was
Hepburn. He had even hired a Hepburn look-alike to work as a mannequin in his
atelier. Looking back it is hard to imagine Hepburn without Givenchy, or Givenchy
without Hepburn. She was his muse incarnate, and after her death he recalled,
"In every collection a part of my heart, my pencil, my design goes to Audrey."

From the first *maison de couture* in the mid-nineteenth century to the fashion
industry of today, the relationship between a designer and his or her muse has been
at the heart of the creative process of fashion design. The muse may be a treasured
client, a beloved friend, or a creative collaborator. A designer may follow a muse for a
season or the relationship may last a lifetime. A muse may have a high public profile
as a celebrity or a film star, or she may be a figure out of a designer's personal past,
summoned back through memory. Like many designers, Christian Dior imagined an
ideal woman for his designs. For further inspiration he turned to his closest coworkers:
Raymonde Zehnacker, who ran the studio; Marguerite Carré, who managed the
workrooms; and Mitzah Bricard, who served as head stylist in the salon. He regarded
them as his "Three Muses," and he valued their opinions, their skill, their intelligence,
and their advice over their physical appearance. Similarly, Yves Saint Laurent relied

Titian, *Pastoral Concert*,
ca. 1509, Musée du
Louvre, Paris

upon the support of two of his closest friends, Betty Catroux, whom he thought of as his "twin sister," and Loulou de la Falaise, who Saint Laurent's partner Pierre Bergé described as Saint Laurent's "creative right hand." Saint Laurent met both women in 1968. Catroux always sat in the first row when he showed his collections, and de la Falaise worked for him from 1972 to 2002. They were precisely the type of women for whom he designed—chic, vibrant, modern—and while they may have not been muses in the conventional sense of the word, they were the women who inspired him.

Many of the men who design for women see a muse as an essential part of the creative process, for as Karl Lagerfeld has wryly noted, "I don't wear the dresses." But women designers can find their muse within themselves, or reflected in the mirror, as seen in the creations of Gabrielle "Coco" Chanel, Mary Quant, Diane von Furstenberg, or Vivienne Westwood. And a muse need not be a woman or even a person. Inspiration can be found in the arts, in history, in the moment, or even in fashion itself. A designer's ideas may even be sparked by a singular desire: to please, to thrill, to shock. As will be seen in the pages that follow, the inspiration behind the iconic designs of fashion history is as rich and varied as the designs themselves. Whatever the source of inspiration, designers are compelled to find their muses, whether the quest takes them to the art museum, to a rock concert, to the cinema, or even to the archives. Or, as Givenchy discovered, the ideal muse may simply walk through the door.

The Classical Muse

Jo Stockton, the bookstore clerk turned fashion model in the 1957 film *Funny Face* (dir. Stanley Donen), was a woman in need of inspiration. For weeks Jo (played by Audrey Hepburn) had posed for top photographer Dick Avery (played by Fred Astaire) at every signature site in Paris. At each location, Dick called the shots, telling Jo where to stand, when to smile, and even what to think. But now they were in the Louvre and Jo took things in her own hands. From the top of the Daru Staircase, hidden behind a colossal Greek statue, she called to Dick, "Just say go." And when he did, Jo ran down the stairs in a sleek red gown, lifting her diaphanous matching cape. With her fleet movements and the cape fluttering above her head, she brought the source of her inspiration to life. Like so many in the fashion arts, Jo had found a muse in the ancient classical ideal.

Ancient classical art celebrates the inherent beauty and natural potential of the human body. The Nike of Samothrace—the statue that inspired Jo Stockton to race down the staircase—gives form to this ideal. The towering stone figure once stood at the crest of a rocky pinnacle on the island of Samothrace in the Aegean Sea. The triumphant posture and wide-spread wings seen against the sky identify the figure as a Nike, a personification of victory. Time has eroded and dismembered the figure, but what remains is glorious; with shoulders pressed back and legs in full stride, the magnificent contours of the body are fully displayed. And the clinging *chiton* that partially covers the body elevates this stunning effect.

The elemental form of ancient Greek apparel clothed the human body but did not disguise it. Cut from rectangular lengths of cloth, the garment had no constructed form. The lengths of cloth draped over the body, and, fastened at one or both shoulders, the line flowed from neckline to hem, only interrupted by girdling at the waist. Excess fabric folded into soft pleats that allowed a range of motion without hiding the body's natural silhouette. Two simple patterns provided infinite variations for a woman's dress: the *peplos*, cut from one piece of cloth and lifted in a fold over the natural waist; and the chiton, cut from two pieces of cloth gathered in at the waist with a belt or band. Unlike sculpture, ancient garments have not survived, so sculpture must provide the evidence. And the striking technique of wet drapery—

The Nike or Winged Victory of Samothrace, ca. 190 BC, Musée du Louvre, Paris

Ancient classical art celebrates the inherent beauty and natural potential of the human body.

GALERIE D'APOLLON

cloth depicted as if damp and clinging to the body's curves—allowed the sculptor to suggest the beauty of a nude form when carving a clothed figure.

Over the centuries, designers have turned to the classically draped figure as a model for styles that pay tribute to the beauty of the human form. There have been deliberate adaptations that were part of a larger cultural moment, as seen in the neoclassical gowns worn in Europe in the late eighteenth and early nineteenth century. Whether associated with Jane Austin's England or Empress Josephine's France, these lightweight gowns—variously called Regency or Empire style—were seen as simplicity itself. Gossamer fabrics in pale colors imitated the natural flow of the classical silhouette in a columnar skirt descending from a snug-fitted bodice with short sleeves and a raised waist.

A century later, in the early twentieth century, the classical aesthetic returned, but this time as part of a singular development in fashion: the release of the body from corsetry. Mariano Fortuny (1871–1949) named his innovative tea gowns the Delphos and the Peplos in tribute to classical prototypes. These one- and two-piece designs were conceived as columns made of jewel-toned silks pleated by a process that Fortuny patented in 1909. And like the Regency/Empire styles of the previous century, Fortuny's gowns skimmed rather than draped the body.

With an inventive approach to handling fabrics, Madeleine Vionnet (1876–1975) bought fashion closer to the classical ideal. Fortuny's gowns, as well as those created in the Regency/ Empire era, were designed as columns; the slim fit suggested the natural silhouette. Vionnet worked directly on the body, draping her cloth on a wooden doll or on a live mannequin so that the lines of the garment were determined by—rather than suggestive of—the body itself. Using light, soft fabrics such as crêpe de chine and silk muslin, Vionnet cut her lengths into shapes ranging from triangles and squares to circles and petals, which she then draped and layered to create the most fluid effects. Her greatest innovation came in 1923, when she cut her fabric on a forty-five-degree diagonal rather than straight along the parallel weave of the threads. By cutting on the bias, Vionnet added a subtle dimension of stretch, allowing her draping to cling close to the body as

Left page: Marion Morehouse (left) and unidentified model (right) wearing dresses by Madeleine Vionnet, photographed by Edward Steichen, published in *Vogue*, October 27, 1930

Left: Madeleine Vionnet's evening dress with leaf belt, 1936

—

The simple lines of classically draped apparel pay tribute to the beauty of the human form.

—

well as unleashing the potential of the fabric's own natural flow. The unity she achieved between body and garment echoed classical precedent. Vionnet designed garments to express rather than enfold movement, for she believed that "When a woman smiles, her dress must smile with her."

Vionnet revived the true classical spirit, but Madame Grès (1903–1993) proved to be the more devoted and enduring acolyte of the muse. Born Germaine Emilie Krebs, Grès studied fine and performing arts in her youth. She had hoped to become either a dancer or a sculptor, but family disapproval, as well as her need to earn her own living, propelled her into dressmaking. She had little training, just a three-month apprenticeship at the House of Premet in 1930. Within four years, she opened her own house in Paris under the name Alix Barton, and, when she married the Russian painter Serge Anatolievitch Czerefkow in 1937, she adopted Grès, the anagram of Serge that Czerefkow used to sign his paintings, as her professional surname.

Despite her limited training, Madame Grès proved consummate in her technique, using draping as the foundation of her approach. Her signature Grecian gowns were made of silk jersey, and she followed the ancient method of working with a continuous length of uncut fabric, shaping the form on a model through folding, pleating, and tucking. She created the graceful flow of her garments by fluting the fabric so that it conformed to the body's lines, narrowing where the silhouette tapered and fanning out over its contours and curves. No one came closer to the effect of wet drapery than Madame Grès. The simplicity of her approach—no layers, no pre-cut shapes, and no understructure beyond an interior ribbon to secure the pleats at the waist—allowed the body to mold the garment. She modestly attributed her intuitive approach to her lack of expertise in traditional technique. To compensate she drew upon her training in the arts: "I used the knowledge I had, which was sculpture."

The gowns she designed in the 1930s paid loyal tribute to the Greek ideal. Most were sleeveless, and she worked with the basic silhouettes of the chiton and the peplos. Necklines generally conformed to one of the three classical types: straight across the collar bones, overlapped, or fastened at both shoulders with a deep plunge to the sternum. But Madame Grès also created distinctive one-shoulder designs. Her pale palette—off-white and oyster, celery green, and ice blue—evoked the aged patina of ancient sculpture. Once brightly painted, the statues were now stripped of all color, lost over centuries of weathering. Her models wore no additional jewelry to distract from the pure simplicity of the classical lines, but her gowns were neither imitations nor recreations. It was as if Madame Grès had picked up the ancient aesthetic after centuries of neglect and seamlessly updated it to meet the needs of her own time and the demands of the contemporary woman.

The war years made it difficult for Madame Grès to continue her practice; the great lengths of fabric that her designs required were simply not available. After the war, she was able to resume her intuitive draping, and she found a ready audience of American clients. Her slim silhouette posed a body-conscious alternative to the voluminous skirts of Dior's New Look, and in the fifties her gowns became a symbol of sensual glamour. Although her designs enhanced the beauty of the body, they hid nothing. To wear them, a woman needed a superb figure and bold confidence. More than any of her silhouettes, the one-shoulder gown best represented the old tradition revitalized for a new era. The woman who wore one—and wore it well—paid tribute to the classical muse through her own transformation into a modern-day goddess.

Evoking the muse was likely on the mind of Jacqueline Kennedy when she approached Oleg Cassini, the designer of her White House wardrobe, for a specific gown for a special event. On April 29, 1962, the president and first lady were planning to host a dinner to honor the Nobel prizewinners of the Western Hemisphere. Passionate about the arts, and well aware of the significance of her public image, Mrs. Kennedy wanted a gown that would express the spirit of the occasion. Both she and Cassini understood the significance of her clothes; whatever she did, everyone watched her. And it only took a single suggestion to inspire Cassini's perfect solution. Mrs. Kennedy mentioned that draped jersey "would be fun for a change," and Cassini recalled the elegant Grecian gowns designed by Madame Grès.

Left: Madame Grès with a gown, photographed by Eugene Rubin, 1946

Below: Dresses designed in 1950 by Madame Grès exhibited with classical sculpture at the Musée Bourdelle in Paris, 2011

Left: Jacqueline Kennedy
with Richard Goodwin
at a party celebrating
the Western Hemisphere
Nobel Prize Winners in
the White House, 1962

Right: Dress by Madame
Grès, photographed by
Robert Doisneau, 1955

Below: Charlize Theron,
wearing Dior Couture,
arrives at the 69th Annual
Golden Globe Awards,
Beverly Hills, 2012

Cassini chose a pale celadon silk jersey; the color, well suited to Mrs. Kennedy's dark hair and sun-tanned complexion, would catch the eye among the men's dark tuxedoes. He draped the jersey into a fluid, fluted column around Mrs. Kennedy's trim figure. The asymmetrical arrangement of the narrow irregular pleats of the bodice simulated the one-shoulder silhouette, but a twisted strap over the other shoulder added a decorous touch to the design. And like Madame Grès, Cassini emphasized the inherent elegance of the classical aesthetic; the gown was free of embellishment and Mrs. Kennedy added only earrings, matching slippers, and elbow-length gloves. As Mrs. Kennedy greeted her distinguished guests and escorted them to their seats, her gown added grace to her movements, and more than one commentator described her as the modern incarnation of an ancient muse honoring contemporary culture's heroes.

Just as the classical ideal of human beauty has endured over the centuries, twenty-first-century designers still find inspiration in the flowing lines and fundamental simplicity of the classically draped gown. Such designers as Yohji Yamamoto, Ralph Rucci, and Isabel Toledo have all explored the inherent grace and freedom of movement that can be attained through draping, but each of them has acknowledged that the pioneering work of Madame Grès played the role of mediator between the ancient world and their own contribution to modern fashion. By following her muse, Madame Grès became a muse herself, showing how to revive timeless techniques and style lines to make dresses that showcase the elemental beauty of human form in motion and at rest.

This is best seen today on the red carpet, where the goddess gown reigns as the favorite style for film stars. The simple yet elegant silhouette moves with the woman who wears the gown, making her camera-ready at every step. And, like the basic template of the ancient Greek gown, the primary concept lends itself to infinite variety. For the 80th Annual Academy Awards ceremony in 2008, Anne Hathaway wore a demure, one-shouldered crimson gown by Marchesa. No jewels were needed to set off the exquisitely draped bodice, embellished with a garland of matching fabric roses. In contrast, in 2012 Charlize Theron summoned up the sensual glamour of Old Hollywood by wearing a gown by

Dior Couture, under the direction of Bill Gaytten, on the carpet at the 69th Annual Golden Globes. With its simple, plunging bodice and trailing skirt, the gown recalled that of the great Nike in the Louvre, whose fluttering draperies reveal and conceal an inspirational ideal of beauty that has not diminished over the ages.

The
Muse in the Mirror

Gabrielle Chanel opened a shop on the most fashionable street in Deauville in 1913. The popular resort on the Norman coast attracted wealthy and stylish visitors, and "Coco," as she was known, already enjoyed a rising reputation as a milliner in Paris for selling distinctively trimmed hats in her own salon Chanel Modes. She was fully confident that she could attract a chic clientele. And, the Deauville shop featured more than hats; it offered a new type of sportswear for women. Chanel particularly enjoyed such seaside pursuits as swimming and lounging in the sun, but found conventional beachwear to be bulky and impractical. So she filled her shop with simple garments and sleek bathing costumes. These were the clothes that she wore, and when she appeared on the beach in her eye-catching sportswear, Chanel proved to be her shop's best advertisement. Her customers were buying more than new fashion; they were seeing themselves reflected in Chanel's inimitable sense of style.

Few modern designers have had as much influence as Coco Chanel (1883–1971). Over a stellar career that spanned the twentieth century Chanel changed the way that women dressed by paring garments down to correspond to the essential contours of a woman's body and accommodate the natural demands of her movements. Simplicity guided her aesthetic, and her innovative vision gave women such modern wardrobe essentials as trousers, the cardigan suit, and the little black dress. Many of her earliest designs still seem fresh today, and no other designer ever sustained as singular a perspective as Chanel. The rigorous consistency of her classic designs was central to her philosophy. For Chanel, the excellence of a design lay in proportion, fit, and function; all else was ornamentation. When she famously declared "Fashion fades, only style remains," she was drawing a distinction between the whims of popular taste and what was true, essential, and absolute in the art of design. Chanel found

Left: Coco Chanel, 1932

Below: Coco Chanel in the French seaside resort of Biarritz, ca. 1928

these truths in her own experience as a woman. She sought her muse in her mirror, and through her distinctive self-identity Chanel discovered the touchstone of style that supported the transience of fashion.

Chanel learned to sew during her two-year stay at a convent school in Moulins (1900–02); she then secured a position as an assistant to the dressmaker Henri Desboutin at the House of Grampayre. But her distinctive sense of style developed out of her circumstances rather than her training. Her relationship with Étienne Balsan, heir to a fortune from his family's textile business, brought her into an elite circle of rich men and stylish women. It is not known how she met Balsan or exactly when she took up residence at

his estate at La Croix-Saint-Ouen near Compiègne, but by 1908 her reputation for distinctive dress began to rise. Unlike the other women in Balsan's life, Chanel had neither family money nor a wealthy patron. As a schoolgirl and a shop assistant she had worn neat, dark dresses with minimal trim at the collar and cuffs. Being small and very slight, these simple, youthful garments suited her far better than the opulent and ornamented styles worn by Balsan's female friends. And, as she came to share Balsan's passion for horses, she adopted the elements of male riding costume so that she could sit astride a horse unencumbered by the voluminous overskirt worn by female riders. Whether she had her garments made by a local tailor or purloined items from Balsan's

wardrobe remains a point of speculation, but by 1908 Chanel had begun to appropriate elements of menswear to fit her own needs.

She also trimmed her own hats, and when the women in Balsan's circle wanted to buy them from her, she persuaded Balsan to let her set up business as a milliner in his Paris apartment. She purchased plain hats—boaters and cartwheels—and added striking but spare ornaments, a clear departure from the heavily embellished styles of the day. In 1910, backed by Arthur "Boy" Capel, she opened her first salon, Chanel Modes, in rue Cambon. Her hats attracted attention when she attended stylish events on the arm of her dashing companion, and soon her hats appeared in the pages of fashion journals, worn by smart young celebrities

and entertainers. But, as she conceived her designs for herself, she was her own best model, as she proved by posing for the pages of the *Comœdia illustré* that fall.

Until she opened the shop in Deauville, Chanel only sold hats, and in the years that followed, the simple and severe aesthetic of her pioneering sportswear served to sustain her growing business through the austerity of the war years. When, in 1915, she left Paris to join Capel, who was stationed in southwest France, she opened her first true maison in Biarritz, providing full design and dressmaking services. Her sleek, tailored daywear—distinctive for shortened skirts and loose, belted jackets with nautical collars and military details—conveyed a serious but sharp attitude that was perfectly suited to the

times. Later that year *Harper's Bazaar* declared that "The woman who hasn't at least one Chanel is hopelessly out of fashion." When fabric shortages imperiled other couturiers, Chanel bought an overstock of jersey from the knit manufacturer Jean Rodier. She transformed the image of this utilitarian material—previously used only for men's undergarments and athletic wear—into a signature fabric, both practical and chic, that allowed her to craft a perfect balance of comfort and fit. In March 1917 *Vogue* dubbed her maison "The Jersey House."

After the war, Chanel moved her headquarters back to Paris, and in the decade that followed she launched innovation after innovation, each one rooted in her personal preferences. By 1917, she had cropped her hair,

Chanel sought her muse in the mirror, and through her distinctive self-identity she discovered the touchstone of her style.

Her sleek, tailored daywear conveyed a serious but sharp attitude that was perfectly suited to the times.

and her slim-fitting jersey suits and tunic dresses projected a new identity for women: energetic, independent, and emancipated. Chanel was, in fact, the embodiment of that identity, and, as an artist, she conveyed her sense of herself through her designs. Her preference for short hair, trousers, and her insouciant adaptation of menswear helped popularize the *garçonne* or "tomboy" trend in the early twenties. Named after the novel *La Garçonne* (1922) by Victor Margueritte, tracing the provocative adventures of a "bachelor girl," the look emphasized a boy-slim figure, comfortable clothes, and a spirited attitude. Chanel's own style drew strength from her bold disregard of traditional gender divisions in dress, and while she did not invent the garçonne look, she helped make it chic.

Chanel exclusively wore her own designs, and in 1921, when she developed Chanel No. 5, it became her personal scent. In 1924, to create her first jewelry line, she removed the gems from her own favorite pieces so that casts could be made for reproduction. From 1923 to 1929, her relationship with Hugh Grosvenor, Duke of Westminster, revitalized her interest in British menswear, and she incorporated the traditional elements of sporting gear—tweeds, reefer jackets, two-toned shoes—into fresh designs for

Left: Coco Chanel in her apartment at the Hotel Ritz, Paris, 1960

Right: Coco Chanel puts the finishing touches on a new creation in her Paris fashion house, 1959

women. The basic vocabulary of a man's suit inspired her cardigan ensemble: a figure-skimming skirt and an easy-fitting jacket was lined with the same silk as the coordinated blouse. And in 1926 Chanel created her most iconic yet infinitely versatile design, a black jersey dress with a high neck, long sleeves, and a figure-skimming silhouette. Even the models who worked in her maison resembled her; they were smaller and slimmer than typical mannequins of the day and most had dark hair. But it was Chanel who best embodied the "Chanel look," for as Loelia Ponsonby, the Duke's fiancée, astutely observed in 1930, Chanel was "The personification of her own fashion."

In 1939, with war imminent, Chanel announced her retirement and closed her salon on the rue Cambon. But postwar developments in fashion drew her out of retirement in 1954. She found the "New Look"—with its corsets, its crinolines, and its yards of fabric—appalling. It was the antithesis of everything that she, as a woman, wanted to wear. Declaring that "Men make clothes in which one cannot move," she revived her signature suit: the slim

skirt, the cardigan jacket, and the blouse that matched the jacket lining. In fact, she had never stopped wearing the ensemble, and, now in her seventies, she proved that that her designs were ageless as well as timeless. And, unlike the ornamental New Look, every detail of her garments had a purpose; buttonholes buttoned and pockets could accommodate such essentials as lipstick, lighters, and keys. The look was fresh, even casual, but it was smart, practical, and indulged her client in the personal luxuries that she favored: superb fabrics, exquisite workmanship, impeccable fit. Although the world had changed, her style endured, and Chanel brought that style back into fashion.

Although most women in the fashion industry would dispute Chanel's declaration that "Dressing women is not a man's job," in the wake of her remarkable return, female designers increasingly sought their inspiration in their personal identity as women. And that distinctive fusion of self and style was best expressed by Diane von Furstenberg (b. 1946) in the jersey wrap dress. The idea is simplicity itself: a two-panel, long-sleeve dress that overlaps

like a dressing gown and ties with a cord. The secret to the design's success can be found in its details: the use of fine jersey that in von Furstenberg's words "sculpted the body," strong colors and graphic prints that give endless variety to a standard silhouette, and style lines that flatter nearly every figure and create a template that can be dressed up or down for any occasion. The concept was practical as well as versatile; the drip-dry jersey made the garment wash and wear as well as wrinkle resistant, whether worn all day or rolled into a corner of a suitcase. Von Furstenberg launched the design in 1972 in an advertising campaign that featured her wearing a print wrap and leaning on a white cube inscribed in her own handwriting "Feel like a woman, Wear a dress!" The wrap dress became an instant classic, worn by women as diverse as actress Mary Tyler Moore, First Lady Betty Ford, and activist Angela Davis. Throughout the decades—including a reissue of the original design in 1997—von Furstenberg has influenced fashion by making and marketing the clothing that she wanted to wear. Like the wrap dress, her source

of inspiration is pure and simple: "What I liked for myself, I wanted to make for others."

Thanks to the bold assertions of Chanel, such contemporary designers as Stella McCartney, Tory Burch, and Victoria Beckham build upon their own identity as women—as well as their distinctive sense of style—in creating their collections. More than just looking in the mirror for her muse, the woman designer knows what she wants and needs from instinct, trial and error, and experience. Perhaps the best example can be seen in the spare yet enticing designs conceived by Ashley Olsen (b. 1986) and Mary-Kate Olsen (b. 1986) for their firm The Row. They came to fame as child actors, and they shared a passion for clothes. But with their petite stature and delicate frames, even designer clothing had to be extensively altered to fit. In 2006, daunted in her search for the perfect white T-shirt, Ashley set out to design one; the result was a slim, smooth, infinitely versatile top made of luxurious material with a single French seam. The Row features classic garments—schoolboy blazers, leggings, shirts, and shells—crafted in exquisite fabrics, with updated proportions and a level of technique worthy of the namesake Savile Row. Rather than a label, the Olsens brand their garments with a tiny gold chain, a reference, perhaps, to the chains that Chanel inserted in the hems of her jackets to make them hang straight. But more importantly, the Olsens learned an essential lesson from Chanel's example: look into the mirror to find your muse.

Left: Diane von Furstenberg, 2003

Right: Diane von Furstenberg, Ashley Olsen, and Mary-Kate Olsen, New York City, 2011

Married to the

Muse

In the summer of 1871, the British journalist F. Adolphus traveled to Paris to report on the state of the dressmaking trade for *Blackwood's Magazine*. The city had suffered occupation during the Siege of Paris and civil unrest in the aftermath of the Franco-Prussian War (September 1870–May 1871), but now there were signs of recovery. Adolphus particularly wanted to interview Charles Frederick Worth but had been warned that the renowned couturier was "as busy as a cabinet minister," so Adolphus was surprised when, within minutes of presenting his card at the elegant salon at 7 rue de la Paix, Worth came out to greet him.

The couturier cordially explained that he had seventeen clients waiting for his personal attention and suggested instead that Adolphus join him for dinner at his château in Suresnes.

The next evening, at the appointed time, Worth's eldest son Gaston met Adolphus at the train station to escort him to his family's home. Worth had just arrived from work and had to change for dinner, but his wife Marie waited on the veranda to welcome their guest. She was dressed in an ensemble of white satin trimmed in lace and black-velvet banding. It was, of course, one of her husband's designs, and it suited her so well that it left the journalist with the

Above: Charles Frederick Worth, 1870

Right: Princess Pauline de Metternich, ca. 1870

Left: Franz Xaver Winterhalter, *Portrait of Empress Eugénie*, 1857, Hillwood Estate, Museum and Gardens, Washington, D.C.

Below: Marie Vernet, wife of Charles Frederick Worth, 1860

lasting impression that "she and her gown were absolutely one." But it was hardly surprising that Marie embodied the ideal grace and sophistication of a dress by Worth. It was Marie who had inspired his first designs and, over the years, she was always there to ignite his imagination; Worth had married his muse.

The British-born Worth (1825–1895) moved to Paris in 1845, and by the next year he had secured a position at the Maison Gagelin et Opigez, the finest silk establishment in Paris. Worth proved to be a talented draper, working with a model—a *demoiselle de magasin*—to display the quality of the fabrics to his customer. Demoiselles wore plain dresses, so as not to distract from the beauty of the silk, but Worth wanted an absolutely neutral backdrop. He made a simple muslin dress for his demoiselle Marie Vernet (1825–1898), and it fit so superbly that women wanted to order the style in silk. By 1850, Worth convinced his employers to allow him to open a small dressmaking department within the maison, and in 1858 he left Gagelin and teamed up with Otto Bobergh to open La Maison Worth et Bobergh, the first full-service, exclusive dressmaking salon in Paris.

Right: Denise Poiret,
wearing a model by her
husband, Paul Poiret,
1913

Right page: Denise
Poiret, Paris, ca. 1925

Worth presented himself as a designer
—*le maître et le créateur*—producing
the styles, selecting the fabrics, and
providing skilled seamstresses to make
the garments. Selling fabrics had been
a man's job, but women had created the
designs as well as made the dresses. It
was so rare for a man to do this work,
that Charles Dickens dubbed Worth
"the man-milliner," but before long his
profession had a new name. Worth is
regarded as the first *couturier*.

Marie also left Gagelin for the
Maison Worth; they had married in 1851.
And she continued to work: as the
head *vendeuse* (saleswoman), the top
demoiselle de maison, and as Worth's
fit model. Every one of his innovations—
the walking skirt, the informal train, the
Princess line—was designed on Marie,
and whenever she appeared in public,
she wore his latest creations. Her beauty
and poise enhanced his designs and
attracted new customers to the maison.
Marie also took an active role in the
business. In 1860, armed with a folio of
her husband's designs, she approached
Princess Pauline von Metternich, wife of
the Austrian ambassador to the French
court. Marie convinced the princess
to order a few ensembles, and after
the princess wore a spectacular tulle
evening gown spangled with silver
stars to an event at court, the Empress
Eugénie ordered her dresses from
Worth. Marie retired in 1865, after a
debilitating bout of bronchitis, but her
reputation as the embodiment of her
husband's vision endured; as long as
Worth created new designs, Marie
served as his touchstone.

Throughout history, male painters
and sculptors have sought inspiration for

their art in the faces and forms of their
wives and lovers. Whether in passion,
affection, or practical companionship,
a life partner could be regarded as
a constant source of inspiration and
support. In this context, it is not surprising
that Marie became Worth's muse. But
he was a man in a woman's vocation,
and in a very real way his circumstance
was unprecedented. And, just as he
redefined his profession, replacing the
modish dressmaker with the all-powerful
couturier, he set another example that
would resonate through the twentieth
century: the fashion designer whose life
companion not only ignites his creativity
but also plays a decisive role in his career.

Paul Poiret (1879–1944) launched his
career in Paris by consigning his designs

to established fashion houses. His
first clients included Madeleine Chéruit
and Jacques Doucet, and in 1901 he
found a position at La Maison Worth,
run by Worth's sons, Jean-Philippe and
Gaston, since the premier couturier's
death in 1895. Poiret soon left in
frustration when Gaston only assigned
him the "fried potatoes" (side dishes,
meaning basic garments) rather than the
"truffles" (the garnish, or luxury wear).
But creating pedestrian attire—plain
skirts, coats, and jackets—led to Poiret's
first signature style, a simple coat based
on a Japanese kimono and impeccably
crafted in a sumptuous fabric. Poiret
opened his own house in Paris in
1903 and began to produce a series
of startling innovations that changed

The press hailed Fath—and his beautiful wife— for burnishing Hollywood extravagance with Parisian sophistication.

fashion history. First he eliminated the petticoat, and then he did away with the corset. Poiret drew upon an unorthodox and eclectic range of sources, including antique drapery, Middle Eastern veiling, and the neoclassical gowns of Napoleonic France. His ensembles were not only glamorous, they were unstructured and comfortable; but a woman had to be slim to wear them.

Throughout the decade before World War I, Poiret created one new trend after another. And the first woman to wear them was always his wife Denise Boulet Poiret (1886–1965). They had married in 1905, and with her slender, lithe figure and her sensuous features, she was the perfect Poiret mannequin. He featured her in design promotions: she was photographed wearing his ensembles, she appeared in costume at the lavish parties that he organized, and, like Marie Worth, when she appeared in public, she always wore her husband's gowns. The designer openly acknowledged her influence, telling a reporter from *Vogue* in 1913 that Denise was his essential inspiration: "She is the expression of all my ideals." When the marriage failed in 1928, Denise took her extensive wardrobe, as well as the meticulous

records that she kept on her husband's designs. The next year, Poiret closed the atelier and discarded its remaining contents. As a result, Denise's garments and notes constituted the most complete account of his work; by sheer happenstance, she became the curator

of his legacy as well as his muse.

As a young man, Jacques Fath (1912–1954) tried several professions before opening his fashion house in 1937. He worked as a bookkeeper and served in the military; handsome and gregarious, he also considered a career

Left: Jacques Fath at work, 1950

Geneviève Boucher de la Bruyére, wife of Jacques Fath, 1948

Left: Giancarlo Giammetti and Valentino Garavani, undated

Right page: Isabel and Ruben Toledo, 2000

Along with his colleagues in couture, Fath struggled through the war years to keep the industry alive in Paris. But in 1946, he took bold moves that brought him to international attention and acclaim. He trademarked his name as a brand, and he produced Iris Gris, his first perfume. And he began to stage spectacular parties; with Geneviève at his side, in one of his dazzling creations, he attracted as much attention as a movie star. A 1948 feature in *Life* magazine described their spring tour of the United States as a traveling fashion exhibition, with Geneviève as a "walking show window for his handiwork." The article, illustrated with photographs of Geneviève in various ensembles, revealed that Fath had created a $12,000 wardrobe for his wife, filling twelve trunks with thirty-five outfits, seventeen hats, and sixteen pairs of shoes. The garments displayed the new hourglass silhouette, with a wasp waist and rounded hips, and the reporter noted that Geneviève "happily needs no padding." Over the next few years of his brief but brilliant career, Fath

in acting. While studying drawing and patternmaking, Fath attended a drama class where he met Geneviève Boucher de la Bruyére (1914–1993), an elegant blonde who worked as a photographer's model. Fath found her captivating; in his eyes, her beauty and style combined "the best of Greta Garbo, Carole Lombard, and Marlene Dietrich." They married on February 18, 1939, two years after he debuted his first collection, and in the

months that followed they appeared at every celebrity gathering, drawing the attention of the photographers with their good looks and glamour. At the Grande Nuit de Longchamp in July, Geneviève dazzled the crowds in a dramatic gown with a tight-fitted bodice and voluminous, asymmetrically draped skirt. The press hailed Fath—and his beautiful wife—for burnishing Hollywood extravagance with Parisian sophistication.

Right: Geneviève Boucher de la Bruyére wearing a black dress designed by her husband Jacques Fath, for their American tour, 1948

—

There is almost no boundary between their artistic creations; they live and work together in a large, open space.

—

worked with other models, including the striking brunette Bettina who became the signature face for his line. But in an interview concerning his ideal woman, he named specific attributes—tall, slim, tiny waist, long legs—then declared with delight, "I have just described Geneviève, Madame Fath."

When Fath died of leukemia in 1954, Geneviève stepped in to run the fashion house and debuted her own collection in 1955. Like Denise Poiret, she found her role transformed from muse to guardian. But other life partners took that role at the beginning of their relationships. Giancarlo Giammetti (b. 1938) met Valentino Garavani (b. 1932) in Rome in 1960. Giammetti studied architecture, but turned his full attention to the rising fashion designer, becoming what he later described as Valentino's "business partner, onetime boyfriend, alter ego, and closest companion" over the course of a fifty-year partnership. His means of inspiration—conferring over ideas, producing the runway shows, and navigating the unpredictable course of the fashion industry in the new century—ensured that Valentino could

work in the best possible and most creative environment until his retirement in 2008. Pierre Bergé (b. 1930) played a similar role in the life and career of Yves Saint Laurent (1936–2008). They met in Paris in 1958 when Saint Laurent had just taken over the helm at the House of Dior. It was Bergé who raised the funds for Saint Laurent to open his own house in 1962, and he remained a steadfast supporter even after the designer's retirement in 2002. Writing in memory of Saint Laurent in 2008, André Leon Talley rightly dubbed Bergé as the designer's "Diaghilev," but more than playing impresario to Saint Laurent's genius, Talley recognized that Bergé, like a muse, was "the one at the heart of his creation."

Few partnerships have combined life, work, and art as seamlessly as that of Isabel Toledo (b. 1960) and her husband Ruben (b. 1961). Both born in Cuba, they met in ninth grade at a New Jersey high school. For Ruben it was love at first sight; Isabel was more attracted to his drawings, thinking that they had been made by his older brother. In the ensuing years, their friendship

bloomed and became a romance. They married in 1984, the same year that they established the Toledo Studio in New York. Ruben promotes and supports the fashion business, but Isabel defines his role as far more inspirational. She does not draw, but when she describes her ideas or even her feelings to Ruben, "he'll sketch it." He helps to design and produce her shows, and he creates the art that graces her boutiques. Ruben even designed Isabel's fit mannequin, modeled on her proportions. There is almost no boundary between their individual artistic creations, and they live and work together in a large, open space. Isabel describes their situation as a "Ma and Pa business model," but more than that, it is a true merging of two artistic talents that are realized in separate but interconnected expressions. There are each other's muses, transforming an old—and often gendered—notion of creativity into a fresh idea for the twenty-first century.

Inspired by the Arts

During a transatlantic crossing from Bordeaux to New York on the SS *Chicago* in 1916, Elsa Schiaparelli met Gabrielle Picabia. Roman-born Schiaparelli had been raised in an intellectual but conservative household, yet she had always been daring and inquisitive, open to new ideas and experiences. Just two years earlier, she had married the theosophist Wilhelm Wendt de Kerlor in London, and they were leaving Europe so that he could lecture in the United States. Like Schiaparelli, Gabrielle was accompanied by her husband, the avant-garde painter and writer Francis Picabia. Schiaparelli enjoyed the simulating conversation with them both, but after the voyage, they went their separate ways. In 1920, Schiaparelli, now separated from her husband, resumed her friendship with Gabrielle, who helped her find her first job in fashion as a saleswoman for Nicole Groult. Despite Groult's excellent connections—she was Paul Poiret's sister—the venture failed. Gabrielle also drew Schiaparelli into a circle of artists that included Marcel Duchamp and Man Ray. Their work offered an alluring alternative to conventional expression by giving free rein to the elusive experience of intuition and dreams. Captivated by this realm of possibility, Schiaparelli embraced their ideas, but rather than painting or sculpture, she chose dress design as her medium.

Throughout her long career, Schiaparelli cultivated a deep connection to the visual arts. She exchanged ideas with painters, photographers, and sculptors. She was a keen patron and collector; wherever she lived, she surrounded herself with works of art and commissioned artists to decorate the

The refusal to insert a line between art and design can have transcendent results.

interiors of her apartments and salons. As a designer, Schiaparelli was certainly not alone in her passion for the arts, but few had ever forged as close a creative link as she did with the Surrealists. She shared their desire to unleash the power of the unmediated imagination and transform the material world into something marvelous. The extent of her collaboration with her artistic colleagues prompted Coco Chanel to dismiss her as "that Italian artist who's making clothes." But Schiaparelli was seeking to dissolve boundaries, not define them. With the fine arts as her muse, Schiaparelli crafted innovative design from a revelatory perspective. She proudly declared: "Dress designing … is to me not a profession but an art."

The parallel paths of art and fashion have often intersected, but the design reform movements of the late nineteenth and early twentieth centuries brought them into an unprecedented alliance. William Morris, whose advocacy of traditional craftsmanship helped launch the Arts and Crafts movement, effectively erased the conventional division between art and design when in 1880 he instructed his followers, "Have nothing in your houses which you do

not know to be useful, or believe to be
beautiful." By the turn of the century,
this concept of unified design, in which
décor and furnishings were approached
as an extension of the arts, came to
include fashion. Progressive design
studios, such as the Weiner Werkstätte
(Vienna Workshop), added fashion
departments, and the ideas of art and
design flowed both ways, as seen in the
work of the Vienna Secessionist painter
Gustave Klimt (1862–1918). Klimt's
companion Emilie Flöge (1874–1952)
designed dresses with slim, unstructured
silhouettes in fabrics influenced by
ethnic textiles. Her striking personal
style inspired Klimt to create his first
gold painting in 1902: a portrait of
Flöge dressed in a blue, columnar gown
embellished with black embroidery and
gold ornaments. In 1904, when Flöge

and her sisters Pauline and Helene
opened a salon in Vienna, they hired
the Wiener Werkstätte to furnish the
interiors and supply fabrics. Klimt
contributed to the salon; in 1906, he
photographed Flöge in the open air
wearing a selection of his own "hanging
gowns." These loose, comfortable
garments—based on the unstructured
design of the caftans that he wore in the
studio—mirrored the lavish aesthetic of
his painting, treating the gown as a blank
canvas for surface decoration.

Color, rather than ornament, inspired
painter Sonia Delaunay (1885–1979).
Around 1910, she and her husband
Robert posited that the juxtaposition
of color in abstract form expressed the
dynamic vitality of modern life. They
called their theory "Simultaneity," and
while they both explored these ideas

in their paintings, Delaunay expanded
her work into textiles, first patching a
quilt for their son Charles in 1911, and
then creating ensembles that they both
wore to go dancing in Paris. In an article
published in the *Mercure de France* in
1914, critic Guillaume Apollinaire listed
the rainbow of colors combined in a
single ensemble: violet, green, sky blue,
tangerine, scarlet, and old rose. "Such
variety," he wryly commented, "has not
gone unnoticed." Initially, Delaunay
sewed scraps on existing clothing,
but she soon developed her own line
of textiles and created simple, sleek
garments featuring bold combinations
of color. In 1925, she opened Maison
Delaunay, a salon in the apartment
that she shared with her husband, and
trademarked the name "Simultané."
That same year, her modernist designs

Gustav Klimt, *Portrait of Emilie Flöge*, 1902, Kunsthistorisches Museum, Vienna

Delaunay expressed the dynamic energy of modern life in the bold juxtaposition of color.

Fascinated with painting and sculpture in her youth, Schiaparelli also imagined that she "could invent dresses."

won wide acclaim at the Exposition Internationale des arts décoratifs et industriels modernes in Paris. Throughout her long and successful career, Delaunay never differentiated between her work as a designer and as an artist, firmly stating that there is "no gap between my painting and what is called my 'decorative work.'"

Looking back in her 1954 memoir *Shocking Life*, Elsa Schiaparelli (1890–1973) recalled her youthful fascination with painting and sculpture—"both of which I did very well"—but she also imagined that she "could invent dresses." In fact, her entry into fashion was almost accidental. After her brief stint as a saleswoman, she was in search of further employment. Among her friends, she was known for her eccentric flair; since adolescence she had created her

own ensembles through alteration and original designs. In 1922, she settled in Paris and began to make clothes for her friends, including Gabrielle Picabia, who encouraged her to seek employment as a freelance designer. By 1925, Schiaparelli found a position in the small firm Maison Lambal, and two years later, she opened a salon under her own name. She quickly won acclaim for her stylish yet unorthodox designs. She created sweaters with knit-in images, including one with a trompe-l'oeil bowknot that proved to be a hit on the international market. She designed a *jupe culotte* (split skirt) that caused a sensation at the 1931 Wimbledon tennis tournament when competitor Lilí Álvarez wore it on the court. She turned out little knit hats, called "pixie" or "mad" caps, which could be manipulated into a

Left page: Sonia Delaunay, 1967

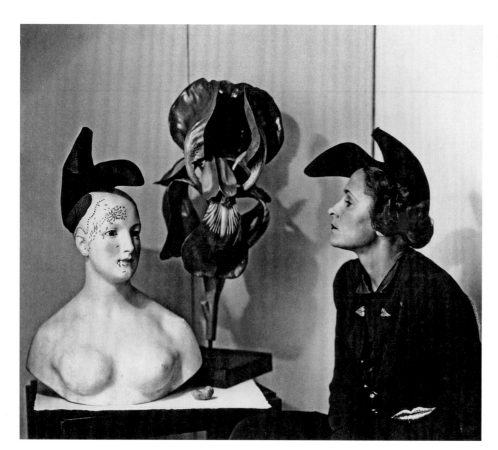

Gala Dalí wearing the
Shoe Hat designed by
Elsa Schiaparelli, 1937

variety of shapes. Her work was elegant yet teasing, sophisticated yet playful, and her most innovative designs drew upon the element of surprise and an impulse toward transformation.

Although unique in fashion, Schiaparelli's vision mirrored that of Surrealist art. The term had been coined by Guillaume Apollinaire, and then explained by critic André Breton in his landmark essay "The First Manifesto of Surrealism" (1924). In a critique of the rational approach to literary and visual expression, Breton urged artists to trust their intuition, their subconscious sensations, and their dreams. The material world, comprehended through a matter-of-fact point of view, limited artistic expression. Therefore, art itself must be transformative, a revelatory process that moves beyond the

mundane into a realm of marvels. While Breton articulated the theory, its core ideas had already appeared in the form of Dada, a reactive "anti-art" movement that loosely coalesced in Zurich in 1916. After the war, many adherents of Dada, including Francis Picabia, gravitated to Paris, where with like-minded artists and writers their chaotic expression of psychic possibility took on greater nuance and sophistication. Schiaparelli encountered the circle through her friendship with Gabrielle Picabia just as she was entering the fashion world. She, too, found inspiration by asking "Why not?" when reason and convention declared "This is how it should be."

From the pictorial potential of knitwear to the tactile quality of fabrics, Schiaparelli made daring and unexpected choices. For evening gowns,

she favored a distinctive rayon crêpe for its rough surface that reminded her of tree bark. She liked the transparency of cellophane and used it to create belts and coats. Prints allowed her to experiment with imagery, ranging from her famous trompe-l'oeil bow to a newsprint pattern composed of legible reviews of her collections. Just as the Surrealists coaxed out the evocative potential of found objects, Schiaparelli used familiar forms, such as peanuts or hands, as buttons and clasps. She encouraged her Surrealist colleagues to design accessories for her salon; in 1936 Meret Oppenheim covered a cuff bracelet in fur, which then inspired her to create her iconic *Object* (*Le Dejeuner en fourrure*), a fur-lined teacup, saucer, and spoon. In turn, Schiaparelli responded to Surrealist objects. Man

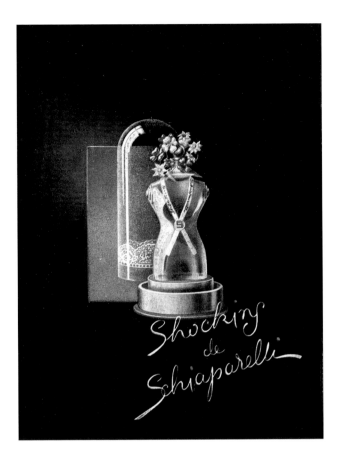

Schiaparelli called her first perfume "Shocking" after her favorite shade of pink.

Above: Advertisement for the perfume Shocking by Schiaparelli, 1943

Right: Elsa Schiaparelli, Evening ensemble, 1937. Linen jacket with embroidery after a motif by Jean Cocteau

Ray's photographs of hands painted by Pablo Picasso to look like gloves, inspired her to craft suede gloves with red snakeskin nails that looked like hands. A photograph of Salvador Dalí with a woman's shoe on his head, taken in 1933 by his wife Gala, inspired Schiaparelli's whimsical shoe hat: a simple high-heeled pump covered in felt—in all black or with a shocking pink heel—to be worn at a rakish angle.

In 1937, as she was designing the film wardrobe for Mae West's role in *Every Day's a Holiday*, Schiaparelli developed her first perfume. She called it "Shocking," the same word she used to describe her favorite vivid pink, and packaged it in a bottle design by Leonor Fini after the ample proportions of the movie star's dress dummy. With her passion for intellectual exchange, Schiaparelli adored artistic collaboration. She embroidered line drawings made by filmmaker Jean Cocteau on to a silk coat and a linen jacket (1937). Her close collaboration with Dalí began in 1936, when his depiction of a minotaur with a drawer in his chest prompted her to design a suit jacket with drawer-shaped pocket welts and pulls for trim. His fascination with lobsters—which he regarded as highly sexed—appeared in her work in the form of a simple, exquisite white organza evening dress

with his sketch of a bright orange crustacean adorning the front of the skirt. Dalí wanted to embellish it further with mayonnaise, but Schiaparelli knew that a dress could not be simply looked at; it had to be worn. And the lobster-print dress was indeed worn, most famously by Wallis Simpson in a photo spread taken by Cecil Beaton and published in *Vogue* magazine in June 1937 to celebrate her wedding to the Duke of Windsor, the former King

Edward VIII of England. Schiaparelli always remained aware that a dress, unlike a work of art, was not created to be consigned to a museum. She sagely observed, "A dress has no life of its own unless it is worn."

By 1940, the looming specter of war dispersed the Surrealist circle, and many artists relocated to New York. Schiaparelli went there too, opening a branch of her salon. Despite the danger,

Right: Elsa Schiaparelli's evening dress with lobster print, 1937

Right page: Wallis Simpson wearing evening dress with lobster print, photographed by Cecil Beaton, 1937

Inspired by the Arts

she traveled between the two cities, returning to Paris 1945 to run her salon until her retirement in 1952. And, in the following years, other designers turned, as she did, to the visual arts to find their muse. Yves Saint Laurent (1936–2008) based his Mondrian dress (1965), a simple yet flawlessly crafted color block shift in wool jersey, on painter Piet Mondrian's rigorous pictorial geometry. Saint Laurent's mother Lucienne had given her son a book on the Dutch painter for Christmas, and while the dress portrays Mondrian's iconic grids, painted between 1921 and 1925, the design transforms rather than imitates the language of the painting. Saint Laurent confined himself to Mondrian's restricted vocabulary: planes of white and the three primary colors, divided by straight lines and right angles in bold black. But while Mondrian worked on the flat surface of a canvas, Saint Laurent had to wrap his planes around a three-dimensional body. The seams shaping the garment were hidden in the piecing of the color blocks, creating the illusion of flatness in a perfectly constructed garment. And the dress reflected an immediate concern in contemporary art. Such abstract painters as Ellsworth Kelly, Ad Reinhardt, and Frank Stella were currently experimenting with color fields, seeking to distill painting down to its

Left: Yves Saint Laurent's Mondrian dress, 1965

Right: A model wearing an Yves Saint Laurent dress with a Pop Art motif at the Centre Georges Pompidou, Paris, 2002

Following double page: Shalom Harlow on the runway at Alexander McQueen's Spring/ Summer 1999 show, London, 1998

By applying the Pop Art images of hearts and faces on sleek dresses, Saint Laurent echoed Schiaparelli's insouciant spirit.

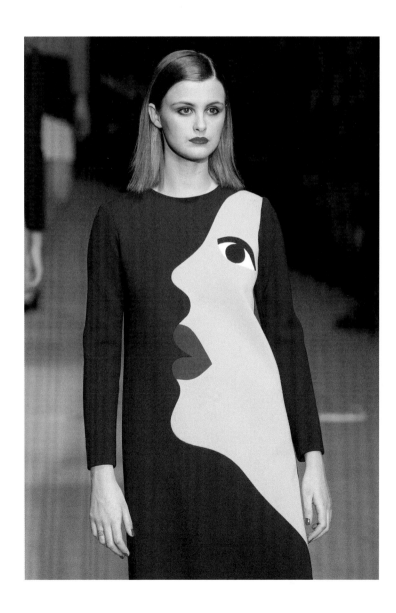

most essential expression. In the years that followed, Saint Laurent explored Pop Art. His bright images of faces and hearts on sleek dresses not only responded to the work of such artists as Andy Warhol and Roy Lichtenstein, but they captured a bit of Schiaparelli's insouciant spirit. With his partner Pierre Bergé, Saint Laurent eventually assembled an extraordinary art collection, acquiring his own Mondrian painting a decade after designing the Mondrian dress.

In an interview in 2012, Miuccia Prada (b. 1949) noted that while dress design was "creative," she did not regard it as an art. While the artist enjoys the greater freedom of a "completely open field," she explained, the designer "must make clothes and they have to sell them." This is precisely Schiaparelli's point in her statement that "A dress has no life of its own unless it is worn." But the refusal to insert a line between art and design can have transcendent results, as seen in the work of Alexander McQueen (1969–2010). McQueen's love of the arts was part of his grand engagement with history, and the inspiration he drew from the history of art was as varied as it was nuanced. He rarely cited a specific work as an influence, but a performance piece by Rebecca Horn, in which blood-red paint shot out of pistols, moved him to create No. 13 for his Spring/Summer collection of 1999. The dress, worn by Shalom Harlow, was simplicity itself: a strapless circle of muslin supported by a belt at the top and tulle skirts below and shaped by a half belt in the back. Harlow stood on a platform that slowly revolved as two robots sprayed steams of color—black and yellow—to create an abstract painting on the dress. As the color sprayed her gown, Harlow moved in response to the streaming paint. Designer, model, and robot painters all collaborated to create a unique garment that was equally art and design. And McQueen made no distinction, for he believed that "what I do is an artistic expression which is channeled through me. Fashion is just the medium." For McQueen, as well as Schiaparelli, fashion may have been the medium, but the arts were the muse.

—

Alexander McQueen declared, "What I do is an artistic expression which is channeled through me. Fashion is just the medium."

—

Shalom Harlow on the runway at Alexander McQueen's Spring/ Summer 1999 show, London, 1998

On February 12, 1947, as journalists and buyers pressed into the salon of a brand new fashion house on avenue Montaigne in Paris, *Harper's Bazaar* editor in chief Carmel Snow brusquely commented, "This had better be good." Her skepticism was well founded. Although the French fashion industry had survived the war, shortages prevailed, and in such straitened times opening a new salon headed up by a relatively unknown designer seemed reckless, even doomed to fail. But Christian Dior was neither untested nor reckless, and his establishment was backed by the textile magnate Marcel Boussac, known in France as the "King of Cotton." The salon fell silent as the show began with the soft rustle of stiffened fabrics. And as the mannequins filed in they swayed and twirled, swinging voluminous skirts layered over petticoats in a display of luxurious abundance that had not been seen for decades. In a single afternoon Dior changed the course of fashion with a collection that he called "Corolle." But his innovative aesthetic acquired a new name when Snow congratulated Dior in a telegram: "It is quite a revolution, dear Christian. Your dresses have such a new look."

But how new was the New Look? In the context of recent fashion, stripped down and spare in response to a wartime economy, Dior's display of extravagance seemed audaciously original, and his structured contours defied the decades-long modern trend toward the natural lines of the body. But rather than seeking newness for its own sake, Dior had created his signature

Above: Willy Maywald, A model wearing Christian Dior's Le Bar (1947), mid-1950s

Right: Christian Dior in his workshop, 1947

Right page: Christian Dior sitting at the desk of his atelier, 1940s

Dior recognized that "everything springs from something else," and with artful insight he took fashion as his muse.

Left: Princess
Pauline Metternich,
photographed by Mayer
and Pierson, ca. 1860–70

Right: Preparing for a
Christian Dior fashion
show, 1947

silhouette in mindful response to the history of dress and the heritage of his profession. It was less a revolution than a revitalization of the taste, tradition, and technique inherent to the original ideals of couture. Dior readily recognized that "Nothing is ever invented, everything springs from something else." And with artful insight, Dior took fashion as his muse.

Christian Dior (1905–1957) cherished memories of his childhood. Born into an affluent haute bourgeois family, he grew up in a decorous, old-fashioned household. In 1910, his family moved from their country house in Grandville, Normandy to a townhouse in the 16th arrondissement of Paris, where Dior first cultivated his taste for elegance in the waning years of the belle époque. He wanted to study architecture, but at his father's insistence

he attended the École des Sciences Politiques. Dior rejected political science as a career, and for nearly a decade he followed a checkered path, traveling, running an art gallery, and doing his military service. In 1934, work as a freelance fashion illustrator opened the door for him to sell his initial designs to fashion establishments; four years later he became a *modéliste* (assistant house designer) for Robert Piguet.

In 1940, military deployment interrupted Dior's work for Piguet, and when he returned a year later, his position had been filled. He secured a similar slot in the more prestigious house run by Lucien Lelong, president of the Chambre Syndicale de la Couture Parisienne. There he worked alongside Pierre Balmain, who noted that "Christian Dior" would be a perfect name for a house of couture. Dior's mannerly

reserve and natural diffidence made him skeptical of self-promotion and ambition. He was content to design in anonymity, but when Balmain left in 1945 to open his own house, Dior became the major figure behind the scenes. And his talent drew notice. In February 1946, Carmel Snow singled him out by name as Lelong's "new designer" and praised the "sensational" collection as "full of ideas." That summer, Dior was approached by the garment industry entrepreneur Marcel Boussac to revitalize one of his flagging businesses, the decades-old house of Philippe et Gaston. The proposition did not appeal to Dior, for he believed that "in a trade where true originality is all important" it was futile to try and "revive the dead."

He offered Boussac an alternative: open a new business, a small, exclusive maison where Dior would have the

Couture was not just dress, it was an ideal of dress, a fantasy of perfection in terms of craft, design, and appearance.

artistic liberty to revitalize the true standards of traditional couture.

Dior's vision of originality was on full display in the sedately decorated salon on avenue Montaigne in his debut collection for 1947. He featured two lines—full skirted and slim—that he named "Corolle" and "En Huit." The shape of "En Huit" resembled a figure eight with equal loops above and below the waist, while that of the "Corolle" recalled an overturned flower with a supple stem rising over full-blown petals. Both had a single source of inspiration: the corseted contours of a woman's body—a high bust, a tapered waist, and rounded hips. To attain this rigorous silhouette, Dior relied on the techniques of dressmaking favored during the rising years of couture: cut, darts, and boning for the glove-fit bodice, and petticoats and padding to support the skirt. And whether slim or voluminous, his silhouettes were constructed in luxury fabrics and lined with taffeta or cambric to give the garment body, a practice that had long been abandoned. In every aspect, he brought back the resplendent ideal of couture defined by Charles Frederick Worth (1825–1895), who had

transformed the role of the dressmaker into that of a couturier.

While both lines employed the traditional techniques and high standards of the best of couture, the "Corolle" designs more fully evoked their esteemed origins. The impeccable fit of Le Bar—a snug shantung silk jacket with sloping shoulders, a tailored collar, and a shaped peplum paired with a wide wool skirt, knife-pleated into a narrow waist band—reinterpreted the elegant Second Empire (1852–70) promenade ensemble known as *costume-tailleur* for a new century. The sharp contrast of black and white, the elimination of extraneous ornament, and the perfect proportions that gave the long, voluminous skirt its buoyant grace seemed to be a natural evolution rather than a revival of the sources that Dior admired. And the vast pleated skirts—*Elle* noted that the shirt-waisted Diorama had a forty-meter circumference, twenty times that of the typical skirt of the day—seemed absolutely revolutionary. *Vogue* editor Bettina Ballard admired the swagger of each mannequin as she strode through the crowded salon, "knocking over ashtrays with the strong

Left: Christian Dior at work, 1950s

Above left: Model in New Look Dior dress, 1947

Above: Christian Dior illustrates skirt-hem length on a model with the help of a ruler, 1953

**Right: Yves Saint Laurent
drawing on a blackboard,
1957**

**Right page: Yves Saint
Laurent for Dior's Spring/
Summer 1958 collection**

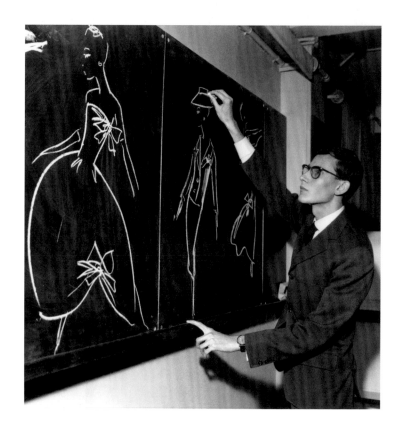

flare of her pleated skirt." After she saw
the presentation, novelist Nancy Mitford
wrote to her sister Diana Mosley "My
life has been made a descent of gloom
by the collections which at one stroke
render all one's clothes unwearable."

The heady appeal of Dior's
luxury lines cloaked the fact that for
nearly a decade designers had been
experimenting with the hourglass
silhouette. In 1939, Chanel created a
wasp-waist suit in velvet, worn with a full
skirt, that she called Watteau. During the
war years, other designers—Cristóbal
Balenciaga, Jacques Fath, Edward
Molyneaux, Mainbocher, and even
Lelong—had featured the curvaceous
contour in one form or another. *Vogue*
instructed its readers in 1945, "The only
thing you must have is a tiny waist, held
in if necessary by a super-lightweight
boned and laced corset," just as Marcel
Rochas introduced the Waspie, a new
corset for a new generation. Dior, in fact,
had been perfecting the idea behind
Le Bar for several years, first in a 1938
design, Rond Point, for Piguet featuring
a long, tapered white jacket over a
flared black skirt. He reworked the style
for Lelong in 1944 as Welcome, now
with a shorter, more snugly fit jacket
and a fuller skirt. Le Bar was created
in the true spirit of couture, with all its
exclusivity and extravagance, for his own
house. With it, Dior positioned himself
as *le maître et le créateur*—Worth's self-
fashioned role—to acquire a legacy that
he felt had languished.

Not everyone admired Dior's New
Look. Several journalists expressed
discomfort with such extravagance
when so many people were still
hampered by economic constraints.
As well as extravagant, the garments
were expensive, and many women, now
used to shorter dresses, chafed at the
dropped hemlines. In July, when Dior
traveled to Dallas to collect an "Oscar"
for couture from the department store
Neiman-Marcus, he was greeted by
protesters from the "Little Below the
Knee Club." Their signs proclaimed,
"The Alamo fell but our hemlines will
not." Dior understood that the aesthetic
of "abundance was still too novel" for
easy acceptance, but he had presented
his collections in the spirit of possibility
rather than practicality, as if a "golden
age had seemed to come again."
While Dior's "golden age" marked the
emergence from a wartime sensibility,

Lagerfeld's brilliant reinterpretation of all the Chanel hallmarks paid homage to the house identity without hiding his own.

—

its true progenitor was the golden age of couture. Worth had transformed dressmaking into an art form, and Dior measured his own work by that standard. Couture was not just dress, it was an ideal of dress, a fantasy of perfection in terms of craft, design, and appearance. And like Worth, Dior regarded dress as a complete presentation, unified by styling from head to toe. From the hats by Lionel Le Grand to the shoes by Roger Vivier, the New Look was a complete look. Dior even produced a line of stockings. In the decade that followed the launch of the New Look, Dior defined fashion. His standard became

the test: whether a designer adopted his ideas, as so many did, or, like Chanel, were inspired to resist them. In taking fashion as his muse, Dior became a muse for others.

Dior's sudden death in 1957 launched the career of Yves Saint Laurent (1936–2008). He had joined the house as a modéliste just two years earlier, and he clearly understood Dior's sensibility. Despite his youth, he was the obvious heir. When thirty of his designs were featured in what became Dior's last collection, the older designer confided to house manager Jacques Rouët that Saint Laurent deserved more public credit. Saint Laurent's initial collections marked a natural development out of Dior's previous lines, introducing innovations, such as the Trapeze line, within the context of the house's

standard aesthetic. But the world of fashion was changing, and when Saint Laurent reflected those changes in designs inspired by the Beat movement and motorcycle gear, the press turned against him. In September 1960, after repeated deferments, Saint Laurent left to serve in the military. He suffered a nervous collapse and was released as unfit; Marc Bohan (b. 1926) replaced him at Dior.

Bohan remained at the head of Dior until 1989, producing lovely yet conservative collections for fifty-seven seasons. Over that time, the house expanded into an enterprise, a path that had been, in fact, set by Christian Dior's own insistence on consistent quality in every aspect of dress from perfume to accessories. And every house was in flux, as a whole generation

Left: Kimora Perkins in a Karl Lagerfeld leather suit for Chanel, 1990.

Above: Karl Lagerfeld and hairdresser Alexandre de Paris checking a model prior to Chanel's Spring/ Summer 1983 fashion show, Paris

Galliano came to Dior with an air of devilish notoriety, creating collections inspired by diverse and improbable themes.

The sweeping skirts and tapered waists echoed Dior's postwar celebration of luxury and beauty.

of founding designers either retired or died. Replacing a famed designer was a daunting challenge, and few rose to it as well as Karl Lagerfeld, who took over Chanel in 1983. Lagerfeld's witty and brilliant reinterpretation of all the Chanel hallmarks—the cardigan suit, chains, braid, tweed, as well as the double-C logo—paid appropriate homage to the house identity without Lagerfeld ever losing his own in the process.

By the time that Gianfranco Ferré (1944–2007) replaced Bohan at Dior in 1989, the house was regarded more as a corporate brand than a traditional maison; Ferré recalled that his initial design brief was "Do some Dior." And the choice to replace Ferré in 1997 shocked the fashion world. When John Galliano (b. 1960) came to Dior from Givenchy, he carried an air of devilish notoriety,

creating collections inspired by such diverse and often improbable themes as the French Revolution ("Les Incroyables," 1984) and the tragic heroine of Tennessee Williams's play *A Streetcar Named Desire* ("Blanche Dubois," 1988). Although he horrified the press with his Spring/Summer 2000 collection "Homeless," in 2007 Galliano struck the perfect note of homage and invention in his sixtieth-anniversary show featuring the lines of the New Look reinterpreted through the lens of Giacomo Puccini's opera *Madame Butterfly*. Galliano's silhouettes echoed Dior's postwar celebration of luxury and beauty, in sweeping skirts and tapered waists. His dazzling palette of color—evoking flower petals and brightly dyed silks—as well as accessories that included lantern-shaped hats by Stephan Jones and

Left and above: Galliano for Dior, Spring/Summer 2007 Haute Couture, Paris

Left: Alber Elbaz, creative director of Lanvin, and Suzy Menkes, fashion editor of the *International Herald Tribune*, at the IHT Heritage Luxury Conference, London, 2010

Right: Christian Dior Haute Couture Spring/Summer 2012 show, Paris

—

The question to ask is how the past spirit of a house can serve as its presiding muse.

—

voluminous *obi* merged his two muses into a seamless fantasy. And fantasy had always been at the heart of couture.

After Galliano's departure from Dior in March 2011, Bill Gaytten (b. 1960), his longtime assistant, temporarily took the helm. His 2012 Spring/Summer Haute Couture collection featured iconic elements of the New Look—decorous elegance, tapered waists, and voluminous skirts—in garments as fresh as they were feminine. His full, floating skirts recalled those of Dior more than six decades earlier, toppling ashtrays in their wake. And Raf Simons (b. 1968), appointed creative director of Dior in

April 2012, has already proven that he can evoke the house muse without hiding his own brilliance.

Throughout the last half century, Dior's deliberate return to traditional couture inspired several generations of designers to move fashion forward. Vivienne Westwood has honored his influence, creating her stunning Metropolitan suit (1995–96) in tribute to Le Bar. Christian Lacroix recalled that as a child he wanted to grow up to be Dior, and in 2007 Saint Laurent acknowledged Dior as his sole "master." But, as Dior noted, "true originality" must fuel design. Otherwise inspiration

devolves into imitation. In an interview with Suzy Menkes in 2010, Alber Elbaz, creative director of the House of Lanvin since 2001, reflected on how the past spirit of a house can serve as its presiding muse. For each season's collection, he creates a story, and only then consults the archive for inspiration. Elbaz cautions against imitation—"been there, done that"—as well as the impulse toward revolution. The right question to ask the archive is virtually the same raised by Christian Dior about couture: "What is it that made this house exist for a hundred years?" Elbaz, like Dior, finds his muse in the answer.

The Muse of the Moment

In 1966, Lesley Hornby, a sixteen-year-old schoolgirl from London's working-class Neasden neighborhood, had her lank brown hair shorn and tinted blonde at Leonard's of Mayfair, one of the city's most elegant salons. To get the expensive experimental cut, she agreed to sit for a photograph that Leonard Lewis displayed in his salon for publicity. A few days later Deidre McSharry, fashion editor at the *Daily Express*, came to Leonard's to have her hair styled, and the photograph caught her eye. Wide-eyed, winsome, and waif thin, Lesley embodied the style of the moment. Her huge eyes, ringed with liner and tiny lashes painted on her lower lids, gave her a childlike appeal; the schoolboy crop that Leonard created emphasized her youthful androgyny. But

her chiseled cheekbones and pouting mouth added a sensual edge to her innocence. McSharry contacted Lesley for an interview and arranged for the paper's photographer to take a few more shots, which she featured in a two-page spread in the *Daily Express*'s February 23 edition under the bold-type headline: "I Name this Girl the Face of '66." The article caused a sensation and transformed a schoolgirl named Lesley into the model called Twiggy, an iconic figure in the youth-driven fashion scene of the Swinging Sixties.

Twiggy may have been the "face" of 1966, but the moment that she so beautifully embodied had begun a decade earlier. In the mid-fifties, after years of postwar doldrums, a new spark of energy could be sensed in London. Fueled by rising optimism and

Below: Twiggy in King's Road, London, 1966

Right: Twiggy wearing a pink dress, 1966

VOGUE

MAI 6 F

REUSSIR
VOTRE ÉTÉ
À COUP
SÛR

EN ROBES DE
COTON ET D'ORGANDI
EN MAILLOTS-SHORTS
ET EN BLAZERS

PARIS

Left: Mary Quant reads a copy of *Vogue* magazine featuring Twiggy on the front cover, London, 1967

Above: Mary Quant, 1965

an improving economy, young artists, designers, and entrepreneurs sought to replace the stoic and stalwart British image—so indicative of the nation's wartime psyche—with a vital and adventurous point of view. The so-called Youthquake had seismic effects in every creative sphere, but its most immediately visible expression was seen in fashion. Countering the traditional image of the tailored gentleman and the couture-clad lady, young Londoners asserted an identity separate from their parents, an identity that celebrated their exuberance, their audaciousness, and, first and foremost, their youth.

The look that they favored was disposable rather than enduring, sassy rather than sophisticated. Daring designers and stylists took their cue from the sharp young "mods" and "dollies" who mocked the dictates of Savile Row tailors and Parisian couturiers and embraced the very evanescence of the moment as their muse.

It took a long time for London to recover from the hardships of World War II. Although rationing ended in 1949, shortages continued for years, and bombed-out sites in central London, cleared of rubble but not yet rebuilt, cast

Left: Grace Coddington modeling the 5-Point bob by Vidal Sassoon, ca. 1965.

Below: Mary Quant having her hair cut by Vidal Sassoon, 1960s

a pall on rising spirits. By the middle of the fifties, however, the slow yet steady turnaround of the economy countered the psychic weight of the recent past, and life in the city began to improve. London's citizens sought to pick up where they had left off prior to the war's disruption, but designer Mary Quant, who was just twenty-one, recalled that young people felt left out. Music venues, restaurants, and nightclubs all catered to an older crowd; if you were young there was "no place to go and no sort of excitement." And daughters were expected to dress like their mothers. Still young but matronly, the queen set the example in her preferences for such traditional designers as Hardy Amies and Norman Hartnell. For more advanced design, chic Londoners followed the template of Parisian couture, and mature sophistication was regarded as essential to style.

But the young population was growing, and the desire to break with the world of their parents launched a grassroots youth movement in style. At first, to define a sense of new identity, the most forward-looking young people turned to ideas from abroad: French film, American jazz, Italian suits. The sharp young men who followed these trends

became known as "mods," after their love of modern music. The close cut of Italian tailoring showcased their lean physiques, but, in a show of disdain for tradition, mods often tweaked their garments, having them tailored to exaggerate the skinny fit, replacing matching lapels with contrasting fabric, or combining

outrageous colors. In 1957, John Stephen opened His Clothes, a Carnaby Street boutique that gave the mods what they wanted, as well as prodding them on to ever more daring styles.

Stephen followed the lead of the mods, but Mary Quant (b. 1934) set the example for their dollies. In November 1955, Quant, her husband Alexander Plunket Greene, and Archie McNair opened Bazaar on King's Road in Chelsea. As Greene later recalled, there were "no clothes in a young idiom to be found anywhere," so Quant and her partners filled the boutique with playful garments and accessories made by young artists and budding designers. Quant had studied art and design at Goldsmiths' College of Art at London University, and her initial role at Bazaar was buyer and shopkeeper. But she had a strong sense of personal style that recoiled at womanly decorum: "I grew up not wanting to grow up." She was put off by the artificial trappings of mature femininity, "the candy floss hair, stiletto heels, girdles, and great boobs." Quant often modified the garments in the store, and she began to create her own designs by manipulating Butterick

Vidal Sassoon
photographed at his
Bond Street salon in
London, 1968

patterns and running them up in fabrics that she purchased at Harrods. At night she studied patternmaking, which enabled her to create original designs.

Quant's muse was youth. She remembered disliking ornate dresses—castoffs from older relatives—that she had worn as a child. She preferred a classmate's clothes; the girl studied tap dance and often wore snug sweaters and black tights. She based her own designs on that clean silhouette and reinvented schoolgirl basics—pinafores and tunics—to suit a young woman's lithe form. Short skirts and high-cut armholes made long limbs look longer. White collars and cuffs added sassy charm. The easy fit skimmed the body in contrast to conventional garments that emphasized corseted curves. For

Quant's clothes, you didn't need a girdle or a structured bra; her designs looked best on a teenaged body that was slim and flat-chested. Each year Quant raised her hemlines; by the early sixties, they landed well above the knees. While it is not possible to attribute the miniskirt to one single designer, it was Quant who made it popular. Quant added schoolgirl flats and colored tights, sourced from theatrical costumers, to finish the look.

From newsboy caps to schoolgirl shoes, Quant created a total look. And she finished that head-to-toe image with a haircut designed by Vidal Sassoon (1928–2012). In 1954, after working at Raymond's in Grafton Street—the owner, favored by socialites, was known as "Teasy-Weasy"—Sassoon opened his own salon and began to reinvent

**Right: Mary Quant's shop,
Bazaar, on King's Road,
Chelsea, London, 1966**

**Right page: Twiggy
wearing a black dress
with a black hat and
pink suede high heels in
Biba's Kensington store,
London, 1971**

hair design. Believing that style should come from the cut rather than setting and teasing, he developed a geometric approach that he likened to cutting fabric. Quant was more than happy to let him experiment, and in 1963, when he gave her a short bob with heavy bangs she brought in all her models to get the same cut. Sassoon advanced from the "Bob" to the "5 Point," a precision cap cut angled up over the ears and the back of the neck with perfectly rounded bangs that drew attention to the eyes. Grace Coddington, the first model to wear the 5 Point, called it remarkable, so precise that no matter "which way you shook it" it fell back into place.

Quant's Total Look set off shockwaves throughout the fashion world; her designs were as significant in the Swinging Sixties as the music of the Beatles or the Rolling Stones. And she enjoyed phenomenal success. A deal with J. C. Penney introduced her to a wide American market in 1962. One year later she introduced her Ginger Group, a diffusion line for department

stores. Also in 1963, the *Sunday Times* gave Quant its International Award for "jolting England out of its conventional attitude." And in 1966, she was granted the Order of the British Empire for service to fashion; she wore a miniskirt to receive her honor from the Queen at Buckingham Palace. Her innovations— the miniskirt, matching tights, PVC rain gear, soft-support seamless bras called Booby Traps—just kept coming, but she always acknowledged that her inspiration came not only from what she thought young women wanted but from what she saw them wear. Sassoon explained that "The street was her atelier." Quant defined her own role as catching "the spirit of the day" and applying it to dress design, "the most significant and speediest of the decorative arts."

Quant's contribution to Youthquake fashion extended far beyond the Total Look. The careers of such notable designers as Caroline Charles, Gerald McCann, and John Bates were launched at Bazaar. The way that Quant ran

her boutique turned shopping into entertainment. Her playful and often anarchic approach to window dressing set the tone from the street, and within the boutique the loud music, late hours, and launch parties made Bazaar a destination for more than shopping. Quant made fashion fast and fun, and within a few years London chic eclipsed Parisian couture. If youth inspired Quant, Quant inspired others to serve the youth market. In 1964, fashion illustrator Barbara Hulanicki (b. 1936) opened Biba on Abingdon Road in Kensington. Although far more affordable than couture, Quant's clothes were well made and costly; at Biba, things were cheap. Hulanicki exclaimed "We practically gave our things away." With a constantly changing stock of skinny T-shirts, cotton smocks, miniskirts, and bell-bottomed trousers, Biba cut across class and economic lines, making cutting-edge fashion available to the widest market. The clothes were not meant to last— often needing repair when worn more than once—but there was always

**Quant filled her
boutique with
playful garments
and accessories
made by young
artists and budding
designers.**

—

**Childlike garments
and unorthodox
poses infused
youth and
prettiness with
sensuality: a
naughty baby look.**

—

something new to buy. And everyone from schoolgirls to pop stars, from working girls to debutantes, could afford to shop at Biba.

Fashion photography added to the excitement of Youthquake culture. Such new young photographers as David Bailey, Brian Duffy, and Terence Donovan—known as the "Terrible Three"—glamorized and sexualized the formerly effete image of the man behind the camera. According to Donovan, their point of view represented their attraction to the new London girl: "We try and make the model look like a bird we'd want to go out with." In contrast to the impeccably groomed image of the fifties fashion model, the new photographers preferred a "morning-after look." Their models became celebrities. Both

Jean Shrimpton and Jane Birkin were conventionally beautiful, but the childlike garments and unorthodox poses and props used in styling the photographs gave their youth and prettiness a sensual edge, a kind of naughty baby look. Through photography, as well as such films as *Darling* (1965), *Georgy Girl* (1966), and *Alfie* (1966), that look came to represent a free lifestyle for young women of modest means who wanted more than school and a job or marriage and a family; many saw modeling as the road to opportunity.

That certainly was the case with Lesley Hornby (b. 1949). But her Pygmalion-like discovery story was a bit more calculated than it appears. In 1965, she began to date Justin de Villeneuve, formerly Nigel Davies, who

had worked for Sassoon. She was a beautiful girl, and she looked just right in the current fashions, so the enterprising de Villeneuve arranged to have her photographed for Leonard Lewis. But the way her career took off surprised even the savvy de Villeneuve. Her raw talent and gawky charm became the epitome of London style, and within a year Twiggy was internationally known and had launched her own line of clothes. With her genuine gamine appeal, Twiggy rode the crest of the Youthquake, but a new wave was already rising. The childlike silhouettes of the Swinging Sixties lost their cutting edge to the ethereal masquerade associated with psychedelic culture. But that's the nature of the muse of the moment—just as you catch it, it slips away.

Left page: Jane Birkin, wearing a short lace nightgown and nightcap, during a photo shoot for *Queen* **magazine, ca. 1965**

Left: Jean Shrimpton posing at a doll hospital in London with a large collection of patients, 1964

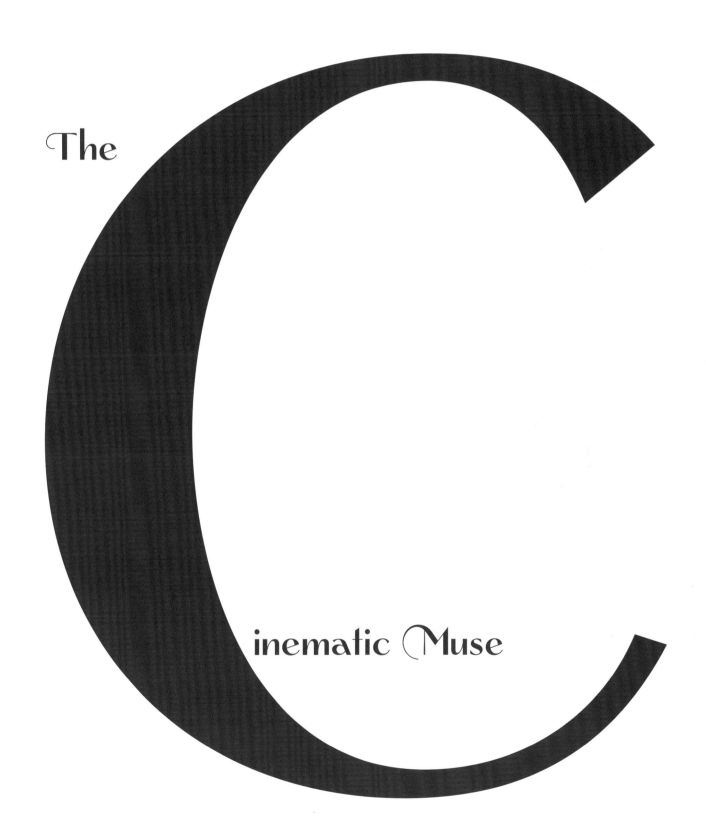

The

Cinematic Muse

When Catherine Deneuve needed a special gown to wear at a royal reception in London in March 1966, where she was to be presented to Queen Elizabeth II, her husband, fashion photographer David Bailey, took her to Paris to introduce her to Yves Saint Laurent at his salon in the Hôtel Forain. Deneuve brought a clipping of a gown that she liked from the previous year's collection, but Saint Laurent created a new design for her, featuring the tunic shape that he had used for evening wear in his recent collections. White, with a high neck and long, slim sleeves, the gown's only embellishment was dark-red embroidery on the yolk and cuffs. The simplicity of the dress did not detract from Deneuve's classic beauty, and the

cut and the embroidery gave the dress a young, bohemian flair. Delighted with the gown, Deneuve invited Saint Laurent to design her wardrobe for her upcoming film *Belle de Jour*.

The relationship between cinema and fashion can be traced back to the early days of film, but there are differences between costume and fashion design. While conventional costume design is conceived as a part of the whole production, inserting a distinctive fashion wardrobe into a film creates as much a statement of identity as that character's lines and gestures. The wardrobe that Saint Laurent designed for Deneuve to wear in *Belle de Jour* as Séverine Serizy, a privileged and proper Parisienne with a secret life of erotic adventure, became part of Deneuve's performance. Each

perfectly tailored coat, elegant suit, and immaculate dress worn by Séverine over the course of the film added to the bewildering complexity of her character. The wardrobe was perfectly matched to Deneuve's cool beauty and understated performance. No other actress—and no other part—would have ignited the same creative spark in Saint Laurent; Deneuve, in the guise of Séverine, became his cinematic muse.

One of the earliest known collaborations between cinema and couture came in 1912, when Sarah Bernhardt asked Paul Poiret to design the costumes for two of her films: *Queen Elizabeth* and *Camille*. Although Poiret expressed a theatrical vision in many of his collections, these films had historic settings, and his costumes were conceived as part of the production rather than an extension of his line. His work went uncredited, but he continued to design for the cinema, creating costumes for four more productions, including *The Phantom of the Moulin Rouge* (1925). In contrast, Samuel Goldwyn brought Coco Chanel to Hollywood in 1931 with the hope that her celebrity would enhance the glamour of his leading ladies. He built a workshop for her with facilities for every aspect of fabrication and hired a staff of a hundred skilled workers, but Chanel found it difficult to adjust to the practical demands of a Hollywood production. She went over budget; costumes for the three main actresses in *The Greeks Have a Word for Them* cost more than

Left page: Catherine Deneuve as Séverine Serizy and Jean Sorel as Pierre Serizy in the 1967 film *Belle de Jour*

Left: Catherine Deneuve is introduced to Queen Elizabeth II, London, 1966

$100,000. She crafted multiple versions of a single dress for Barbara Weeks to wear in *Palmy Days* for different positions and camera angles. And, on the set of *Tonight or Never*, she crossed swords with superstar Gloria Swanson, prompting Swanson to accuse Chanel of not knowing how to design for film. Chanel left Hollywood feeling that her work was neither understood nor appreciated; her clothes would appear in such French films as *The Rules of the Game* (1939) and *The Umbrellas of Cherbourg* (1964), but rather than exclusive designs, the garments were selected from house collections.

Elsa Schiaparelli had a very different attitude about working in cinema. She happily collaborated on a number of productions, including *Topaze* (1933) and *Moulin Rouge* (1952), and she believed that cinema would have an estimable impact on fashion, exclaiming, "What Hollywood designs today, you will be wearing tomorrow." Whether or not that proved true, the public did respond to the iconic power of costume. Women's trousers became the height of sophistication when Travis Banton dressed Marlene Dietrich's sultry singer Amy Jolly in a custom-fit tuxedo in *Morocco* (1930). Such serviceable garments as T-shirts and leather jackets acquired sex appeal when worn by Marlon Brando in *A Streetcar Named Desire* (1951) and *The Wild One* (1953).

**The image of
Monroe's skirt
billowing up
from a gust from
a steam vent
made an indelible
impression.**

The image of Marilyn Monroe standing on a subway vent in a pleated white halter dress designed by William Travilla was so indelible that most audiences believed that they saw it in the film *The Seven Year Itch* (1955). The famous image was, in fact, a publicity still; in the actual film, the audience only saw Marilyn's head and upper body as she cooed "Isn't it delicious?" And after designer Helen Rose dressed Elizabeth Taylor in a full slip as Maggie the Cat in *Cat on a Hot Tin Roof* (1958), that pedestrian garment was never the same. In each of these examples, however, it was the star, rather than the design or the designer, that gave the costume its power. The costumes showcased the celebrity's personality, which, in turn, vitalized the character on the screen.

Many actors forged strong relationships with their costume designers. Travilla, who met Monroe in 1952 and sewed her into a skin-tight gold gown for *Gentlemen Prefer Blondes* in 1953, dressed her for public appearances. But she always appeared as "Marilyn," a carefully cultivated image that blurred her own identity with her film persona. After dressing Elizabeth Taylor and Grace Kelly in a number of films, Helen Rose designed their wedding gowns. Perhaps the most enduring bond was between Audrey Hepburn and Hubert de Givenchy. For their first collaboration, the film *Sabrina* (1954), Hepburn selected garments from his previous year's collection; Edith Head retained full credit for costume design. And while he created Hepburn's

Left: Marilyn Monroe wearing the gold lamé gown designed by Bill Travilla in a publicity still for *Gentlemen Prefer Blondes* (directed by Howard Hawks), 1953

Above: Marilyn Monroe standing on a subway grate wearing a gown by Bill Travilla in a publicity still for *The Seven Year Itch* (directed by Billy Wilder), 1954

wardrobe for her subsequent films, it was not until *Charade* (1963) that Givenchy received solo credit as the costume designer. Even in *Breakfast at Tiffany's*, with its unforgettable image of Hepburn's fragile sophisticate Holly Golightly in that little black dress, Givenchy was only responsible for "Miss Hepburn's principle wardrobe"; Pauline Trigère designed the wardrobe for Patricia Neal, with Edith Head credited as "costume supervisor."

For Yves Saint Laurent (1934–2008), the stage rather than the cinema was the genesis of his interest in costume design. In 1950, he saw a performance in Oran, his boyhood home in Algeria, of Molière's *L'École des femmes*, costumed by the famed fashion illustrator Christian Bérard. Four years later, seeking career advice from Michel de Brunhoff, editor in chief of *Vogue* Paris, Saint Laurent expressed a strong desire to design theatrical sets and costumes, although, he confessed, "I am extremely drawn to fashion." In 1955, after moving to Paris, Saint Laurent took his sketches

to Michel de Brunhoff. Declaring that "Never in my life have I met anyone so talented," de Brunhoff arranged an introduction to Dior, who hired Saint Laurent on the spot. Saint Laurent's meteoric rise left him no time to indulge his early theatrical aspirations, but in 1959, after taking up the reins of the House of Dior and introducing his revolutionary Trapeze line, Saint Laurent welcomed the opportunity to design costumes for Roland Petit's ballet *Cyrano de Bergerac*. Over the next few years, Saint Laurent enjoyed further collaborations with Petit, and he also created costumes for films, including the wardrobe for Claudia Cardinale in *The Pink Panther* (1963).

Catherine Deneuve (b. 1943) came to Saint Laurent's salon at a crucial time. The world of fashion was in flux; boutiques were luring younger customers away from the traditional couture houses and London had eclipsed Paris as the source of cutting-edge design. Saint Laurent had tired of the rigorous conventions of couture.

As the head of his own maison, he increasingly turned to unorthodox sources for inspiration—beatniks, work clothes, military uniforms—often getting harsh reviews, and he wanted to reach a broader clientele, tartly stating, "I am fed up with making dresses for blasé millionaires." On September 19, 1966, he opened his own boutique, Saint Laurent Rive Gauche, near the Latin Quarter. As the guest of honor, Deneuve wore an exquisite military-style coat, simply accessorized with oval sunglasses and a black velvet hairband. Her garments were designed by Saint Laurent, but they were neither part of the recent fall/winter collection that included such highlights as his "Pop Art" dresses and his first Le Smoking tuxedo, nor from the line featured in the boutique. Deneuve was about to start filming *Belle de Jour*, and her demure ensemble gave the public their first glimpse of the wardrobe designed for Séverine Serizy.

Spanish film director Luis Buñuel based his script on a 1928 novel by Joseph Kessel. Séverine is the wife of Pierre, a good-hearted, handsome, and successful physician—his louche friend Henri Husson calls him a "boy scout"—and she has everything she needs: love, security, and material wealth. Yet, she avoids sexual intimacy with her kind and devoted husband, escaping instead into erotic and often masochistic fantasies. When Husson slyly mentions a mutual acquaintance who secretly works in a brothel, Séverine feels compelled to go there, and soon she spends every afternoon, from two to five, as a prostitute called Belle de Jour. But one of her clients, a repellant young thug, becomes obsessed with her, eventually tracking her to her lavish apartment, terrorizing her, and then attacking Pierre, who is left paralyzed and blind. Throughout it all, Deneuve's Séverine remains shockingly passive, with only an occasional flicker of fear marring her flawless composure.

Saint Laurent conceived Séverine's wardrobe as a reflection of her privileged life, but also as the attire of her public persona. The garments that she wears

Following double page:
Catherine Deneuve and
Jean Sorel on the set of
Belle de Jour, 1967

Luis Buñuel's
Masterpiece of Erotica!

ROBERT and RAYMOND HAKIM
present

Belle de Jour
(BEAUTY OF THE DAY)

with CATHERINE DENEUVE

WINNER BEST PICTURE
VENICE FILM FESTIVAL

—

**The designs were
original, derived
neither from Saint
Laurent's recent
collections nor
his line for Rive
Gauche.**

—

Left page: Audrey Hepburn
on location on Fifth Avenue
in New York during the
filming of *Breakfast at
Tiffany's* (directed by Blake
Edwards), 1961

Above: Poster for *Belle
de Jour* (directed by Luis
Buñuel), 1968

Right: Yves Saint Laurent
with actress Catherine
Deneuve, 1968

What began as an artistic collaboration evolved into enduring friendship, and off screen Deneuve wore garments by Saint Laurent.

are couture in quality, but the designs were original, derived neither from his recent collections nor his line for Rive Gauche. Deneuve would later reflect that while other designers "make sure their clothes are always identifiable" in a film, Saint Laurent exhibited an unparalleled "modesty," crafting clothes that advance the expression of character. For Séverine, he created an immaculate, tailored look: a perfectly feminine military coat in slate-gray wool with a matching *tambourin*; a neat sand-toned zip-front dress with long sleeves and dropped waist; a severe black schoolgirl frock with white cuffs and collar. Some of the elements echo earlier lines—the military detail of pea coats (Spring/Summer 1962), white collars on dresses (Spring/Summer 1963), the safari aesthetic (Spring/Summer 1966)—but when worn by Deneuve in character they add to the sense that this is the wardrobe of a

real woman who has made deliberate choices in everything she wears. Every detail adds to that character. In an era of rising hemlines, Séverine's skirts rise just to her knees, fashionable but not too short. Her hats and gloves match her coat; she wears high-quality, low-heeled pumps in patent-leather

by Roger Vivier. Her lingerie is white and unadorned, a striking contrast to the provocative garments worn by the other women in the brothel. And her one daring garment—a shiny patent-leather trench coat—is modestly cut, buttoned up, and belted. Like Séverine's enigmatic personality and impassive demeanor,

these exquisite garments created an impenetrable surface that both protected and disguised her.

When *Belle de Jour* was released in 1967, Hélène Nourry was credited with the costume design; Saint Laurent had only created the wardrobe for Deneuve. He would dress her again—*La Chamade* (1968), *Mississippi Mermaid* (1968), and *The Hunger* (1983)—and when Deneuve worked with other designers, she found that they fell short of his standard. She believed that more than any other designer Saint Laurent created character through his costumes, and his wardrobe eased the artistic challenge of becoming "the someone else an actress has to be." What began as an artistic collaboration evolved into enduring friendship, and when he died Deneuve paid tribute to their most memorable co-creation. She attended his funeral on June 5, 2008, in a shiny black coat and patent-leather pumps; with her arms filled with martyr's palms, she once again embodied his cinematic muse, Séverine Serizy.

Left page above: Catherine Deneuve attends Yves Saint Laurent's funeral service on June 5, 2008 at Église Saint-Roch in Paris

Left: Catherine Deneuve and Jean Sorel in *Belle de Jour*, 1967

Right: Catherine Deneuve in *The Hunger* (directed by Tony Scott), 1983

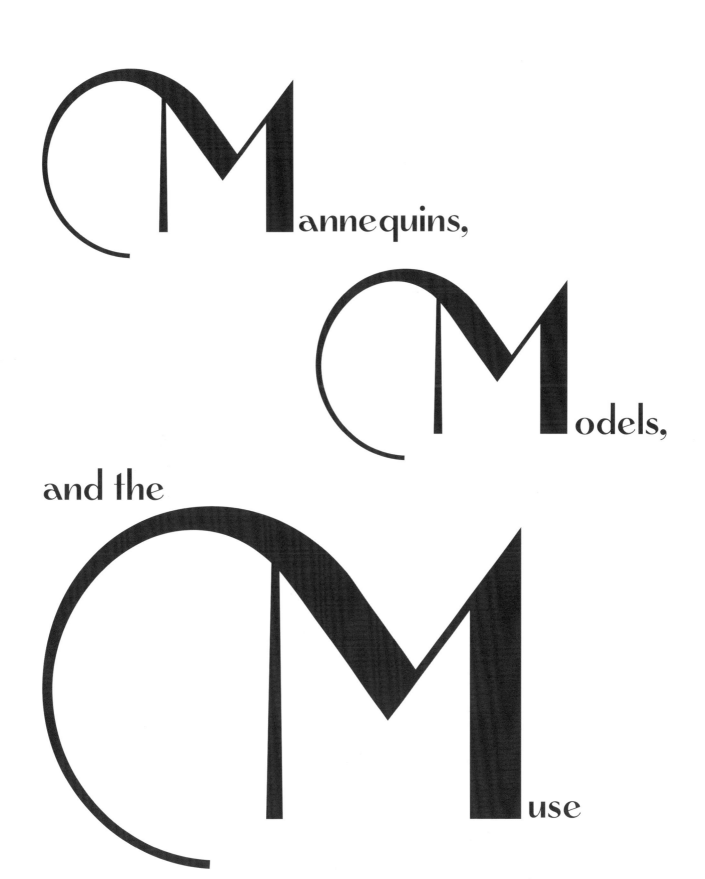

Mannequins, Models, and the Muse

A vaporous burst of light pierced the darkness that engulfed the runway. To the astonishment of the audience gathered to see Alexander McQueen's "Widows of Culloden" collection (Fall/Winter 2006–07) in Paris, the luminous wisp began to swirl and expand until a shadowy figure emerged. It was a woman dressed in fluttering tiers of ivory organza, and as her body floated midair, moving gracefully to the poignant strains of the theme from *Schindler's List*, the audience recognized her as Kate Moss. But in fact, it was not Moss on the runway but her image. The breathtakingly beautiful phantom was a hologram, filmed in advance of the show. And as the figure dissolved back into the wisp of light and then faded into the darkness, it seemed as if some magical force had materialized over the runway and then slipped out of sight. Like an apparition—bewildering yet beguiling—it had held the audience spellbound. Had they seen an extraordinary collaboration of a designer and his model? Or had they witnessed the appearance of his muse?

Today, models are the face of fashion. With their distinctive looks, enviable proportions, and inimitable walks, they present a designer's idea to the industry and to the wider world. We see them on magazine covers, billboards, and on the red carpet, setting a standard of beauty and style to which we can only aspire. It is natural, then, to assume that in the world of haute couture the model serves as the incarnation of the muse. But the celebrity status of the twenty-first-century model has humble origins in the pedestrian profession of the nineteenth-century mannequin. And, for many designers, throughout the history of couture, the model has served in precisely that capacity: as a figure to fit and a form for display. Christian Dior, who insisted on personally interviewing every model hired by his maison, did not involve his "mannequins" in the initial stages of design. Sketching, cutting, and the toile came first, and while he stated, "My mannequins are what gives life to my dresses," their role was to animate the finished design rather than inspire the idea. For some designers, models have played the role of muse, but more typically the model inspires the stylist and the photographer after the designer's work is done. And while McQueen had his share of muses, the magical moment he staged with Moss on the runway was less an homage to her than to the mystery of creative inspiration.

—

With their distinctive looks and inimitable walks, models present a designer's idea to the wider world.

—

Right: A holographic image of Kate Moss is projected during Alexander McQueen's Fall/Winter 2006–07 Ready-to-Wear collection show in Paris, 2006

Left: Christian Dior adjusts the dress on a model in his Paris salon in preparation for the Spring Collection debut, 1957

Above left: Left: A black brocade and rose-taffeta opera cloak designed by Lady Duff Gordon, worn over a silver lace dress.

Above right: A moleskin coat worn with a classical headdress, 1915

Until the mid-twentieth century, in the vocabulary of fashion, *le modèle* referred to a unique design and *le mannequin* to the woman who modeled it. This derives from a dressmaking practice, traced to fifteenth-century France, in which a dressmaker provided a sample garment in miniature on a doll—or mannequin—to privileged clients. By the eighteenth century, the custom became a convention among the top tier dressmakers; in general mannequins were a third life-size or less and made of wicker. Wirework replaced wicker in the 1830s, which in turn, was supplanted by papier mâché, crafted near life-size

and augmented with wax faces, arms, and legs. Also, by the mid-nineteenth century, exclusive fabric establishments employed *demoiselles de magasin*, good-looking female sales assistants upon whom the male drapers could "demonstrate" their wares. While working at Gagelin et Opigez, the finest silk mercer in Paris, Charles Frederick Worth met and then married the demoiselle Marie Vernet; at his own maison, Worth et Bobergh, Marie served as his primary fit model. She also wore his creations to public events to attract new clientele.

Marie Worth was her husband's fit model, top *vendeuse*, and best

advertisement, as well as his muse. But she was not a mannequin. Worth did employ living mannequins to stage in-house tableaux for sales promotion and to introduce new lines. But it was Lucy, Lady Duff Gordon (1863–1935), who first conceived the novelty of the "mannequin parade," the forerunner of the runway show. She came to prominence in London in the 1890s under the name "Lucile," creating garments with such provocative names as "Twilight and Memories" and "Sighing Sounds of Lips Unsatisfied." Her "Gowns of Emotion" were displayed by a group of handpicked mannequins. They were

all tall, and Lucile drilled them in posture and deportment to mirror the patrician habits of her clientele. She also gave them glamorous stage names—Hebe, Gamela, Dolores—and she took her mannequin parades on tours to the continent and to the United States. By the turn of the century, most fashion houses had a *cabine* or in-house studio of mannequins whose duties included fitting and modeling. Their function differed little from the inanimate mannequins that they superseded. In 1925, Paul Poiret fended off a curious journalist who wanted to interview his mannequins: "Do not speak to the girls. They are not there." And when top designers photographed their works, they favored socialites, stage and screen stars, and, if possible, royalty over their mannequins, or, in the case of Chanel, posed themselves.

In his 1956 career memoir, *Christian Dior et moi*, Dior affectionately wrote about the mannequins in his cabine: slender Odile, who passed the time devising elaborate menus to cook for her husband; petite Victoire, whose gamine appearance embodied the spirit of youth; sultry Alla, whose strong features evoked "the mysterious allure of the East." Of all the mannequins, Renée best personified Dior's ideal. But aside from noting that her "proportions resemble those of my imagination," he did not describe her; rather, with every new design she was "reincarnated," so that "one sees not her face but the living creation." Dior cautioned his readers not to believe in the cliché of an inspired designer draping a brand-new creation directly on a mannequin. Sketching, planning, and cutting came first, and the mannequin—first to fit, and then to display—entered later in the creative process. He also differentiated between the "successful" mannequin, who possesses the flair to "carry off" a dress, and the "inspiring" mannequin, who comprehends "the mood, tradition, and line of a dress from the instant of its creation." There is no doubt that Dior preferred the "inspiring" mannequin; but unlike a muse, her role was to facilitate the idea rather than ignite it.

Left: David Bailey gives instructions to Jean Shrimpton during a photo shoot, 1964

Right: David Bailey sets up a shot of Jean Shrimpton, ca. 1963

In the 1950s, notably in the United States, such models as Dorian Leigh, Sunny Hartnett, Suzy Parker, and Dovima gained fame in their own right, posing for photographs rather than working in the salon or walking the runway. Unlike mannequins in a designer's cabine, these models forged direct creative relationships with editors of the top fashion journals and such famed photographers as Irving Penn and Richard Avedon. This is the romantic premise of the 1957 film *Funny Face*, in which the photographer rather than the designer transforms plain Jo Stockton (Audrey Hepburn) into a "bird of paradise." Editor Maggie Prescott (Kay Thompson) is seeking a new, more intellectual image for *Quality* magazine, but the photographer, Dick Avery (Fred Astaire), becomes frustrated when he tries to shoot a model—played by Dovima as a hilarious dimwit—alongside a modern sculpture. He takes his crew to a bookstore and discovers Jo, a beatnik sales girl. They all go to Paris, where Paul Duval (Robert Flemyng),

"the most important designer in Paris," has created a whole collection for "The *Quality* Woman," and in a glorious fashion montage, art directed by Richard Avedon, Dick shoots Jo in Duval's designs. As the designer, Duval has a relatively minor role. He does not see Jo until the collection is completed, and while the photographs are superb, the runway show is a disaster. Duval, like Dovima's model, is played for laughs. He is imperious, but his clothes are gorgeous. And that's hardly surprising; they were designed by Hubert de Givenchy for his very own muse.

The image of the Swinging Sixties was as much a creation of London's top photographers—David Bailey, Brian Duffy, and Terence Donovan—as its designers. Mary Quant described Jean Shrimpton (b. 1942) as "the most beautiful of all the models I have known," and "The Shrimp" with her English rose complexion, thick mane, and coltish legs embodied the perfect look for Quant's designs, but it was Bailey who crafted Shrimpton's image and

launched her career. He had a series of model-muses, and, in turn, inspired the character of the intense—and intensely attractive—photographer in Michelangelo Antonioni's film *Blow-Up* (1966). Thomas (David Hemming) is at the center of the fashion world, and young women hope to climb into his bed as well as pose in front of his camera. Such popular models as Verushka and Jane Birkin appear in the film. Obsession with models is the premise for William Klein's film *Qui êtes-vous, Polly Maggoo?* (1966). Model Dorothy MacGowan plays Polly, who is pursued by everyone from a television presenter to a prince, as well as the press and the public. The film opens with an outrageous runway show featuring a space-age sheet-metal collection by "genius" designer Isidore Ducasse (Jacques Seiler). The beleaguered models, including MacGowan and Donyale Luna, are bolted into garments that restrict their movements and cut their skin.

Model Peggy Moffitt (b. 1939) appeared in both films, but in her

Peggy Moffitt viewed her relationship with Rudi Gernreich as a catalyst: "We played aesthetic ping-pong."

Above: Pat Cleveland and Halston at Halston's studio in New York City, 1972

Right: Peggy Moffitt and Rudi Gernreich, undated

off-screen career she truly played the muse to designer Rudi Gernreich (1922–1985). Moffitt was working as an actress, as well as a model, when Gernreich, a well-established designer, asked if she could find the time to be his fit model for a new junior line. She recalls an instant creative connection. Gernreich found her long-limbed dancer's body perfect for the simple silhouettes, short skirts, and bold prints that formed the core of his junior line. With her husband William Claxton behind the camera, the trio created some of the most innovative looks in fashion, including the topless bathing suit, or monokini (1964). Moffitt's lithe

yet angular poses added quirky cutting-edge verve to Gernreich's striking designs. His bold, graphic designs inspired her idiosyncratic makeup; the eye lines that she painted were the most extravagant and artistic in contemporary fashion. They even made a film together: *Basic Black* (1967), shot by Claxton; but there was no narrative, only Moffitt, Léon Bing, and Ellen Harth striking quirky poses in Gernreich's marvelous designs. Looking back at their years of collaboration, Moffitt confessed that without one another they still would have found success. But together they achieved more than either expected: "We were each other's catalyst. We didn't invent each other—we played aesthetic ping-pong."

The face of fashion literally changed in 1966 when *Vogue* declared that Donyale Luna was the "Model of the Year." She was the first model of African heritage to appear on the cover of a fashion magazine: the January 1965 issue of *Harper's Bazaar* in a sketch by Katharina Denziger and then the March 1966 issue of British *Vogue* in a photograph by David Bailey. Over the next decade more women of color, notably Naomi Sims and Beverly Johnson—posed in fashion shoots and

Left: Peter Lindbergh's
Faces of Fashion:
Naomi Campbell, Linda
Evangelista, Tatjana
Patitz, Christy Turlington,
and Cindy Crawford, 1989

Above: Karl Lagerfeld
and Stella Tennant, 2003

walked the runway, and in the early eighties Iman became the highest-paid model in history. But the racial imbalance in the field continued. At the same time, appreciation for unorthodox or ethnic-looking women—Marisa Berenson, Penelope Tree, Verushka—developed, further challenging the singular European standard of beauty. Models also gained in celebrity status, appearing along with movie stars and socialites at top clubs and Hollywood premiers. The designer Halston, born Roy Halston Frowick (1932–1990), hobnobbed with his high-profile clientele—Liza Minnelli, Elizabeth Taylor, and Bianca Jagger—but he rarely went anywhere without a glamorous entourage of models, including Angelica Huston, Alva Chinn, and Pat Cleveland. The "Halstonettes," a term coined by André Leon Talley, were seen as often at chic parties and Studio 54 as on the runway. But rather

than muses who inspired the designer to create designs, they brought those designs to life. And their celebrity was soon eclipsed by the rise of the "Supermodels." The so-called Trinity, Linda Evangelista, Naomi Campbell, and Christy Turlington, as well as Claudia Schiffer and Cindy Crawford, gained autonomous fame, so much so that the public paid as much attention to them as to what they were wearing.

In the late nineties, David Bailey interviewed several designers for his book *Models: Close-Up* (1999). When asked if he relied upon a muse for inspiration, Karl Lagerfeld responded, "You know, I don't wear the dresses I design." He explained that imagining his models helped him establish the mood for his collection. Lagerfeld named his current favorites: Stella Tenant, Karen Elson, and always Lady Amanda Harlech. And as for Supermodels?

The model may impersonate the muse, but the muse itself remains a mystery.

"They take attention away from fashion." Isaac Mizrahi also said that he designs with his models in mind: "They become part of my psyche, like little seraphic voices in my head saying This is what I want. Put me in this dress.'" Bailey didn't speak with McQueen, and McQueen left no explanation about Kate Moss's ghostly appearance in 2006. And five years later Moss wore the dress again, in a photographic tribute to the late designer for the May 2011 issue of British *Harper's Bazaar*. The photograph presents the iconic image of a model: a beautiful woman in a beautiful dress. But the magic is gone; her face is clearly seen, and her body has substance. Like the very essence of inspiration, McQueen's flickering display was ephemeral, meant to move the artist to make something lasting before the idea faded into darkness. And, while the model may impersonate the muse, the muse itself remains a mystery.

Left: Kate Moss and British designer Alexander McQueen, 2004

Right: Kate Moss models for Alexander McQueen, 1996

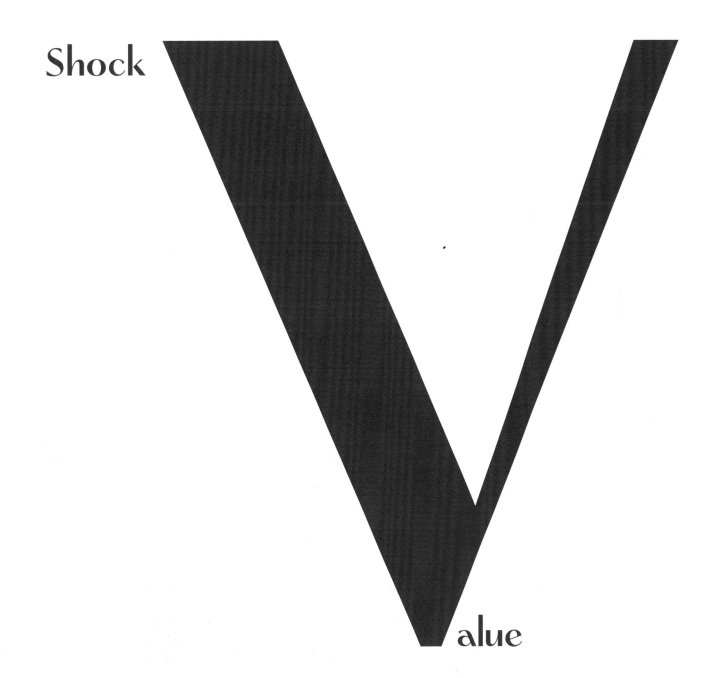

Shock Value

The crisp shirts and tailored trousers of Maison Martin Margiela's Spring 2011 Ready-to-Wear collection delivered the theme as promised in the program notes: "Men's wardrobe meets the woman's body." The famously private Margiela—who rarely grants interviews or poses for photographs—had left the maison two years earlier, but the house designers had fully assimilated his signature deconstructive approach to design. Along with immaculate construction and classical styling, the initial garments on the runway featured the subtle manipulation of contour lines. A smooth panel of fabric from the shoulder to the hem obscured the back of the jackets and the shirts; shirtsleeves were augmented with a tucked extension running the length from armhole to

cuff. And, as the show unfolded, the silhouettes of the garments further flattened until they were reduced to a set of two-dimensional planes that encased each model's body. The impeccably crafted details were right but the spatial conception was shockingly wrong. These faultlessly tailored garments subverted the assumption that clothing must be made in three dimensions. Everyone who viewed the garments had to wonder: When is a shirt no longer a shirt?

Throughout history, artists in every field have recognized the aesthetic value of shock. Monuments to ancient gods were carved on a gigantic scale so that mere men and women would always be aware of the difference between themselves and the divine. Illusionist painting made it appear that the ceilings

of Renaissance churches opened to the sky, giving awestruck worshippers a glimpse into heaven. Sculptors transformed such hard materials as marble into the likeness of supple, undulating flesh that seemed as capable of movement as their own. In each case, what is seen runs contrary to what is known, and that triggers a frisson of shock. What baffles the mind stimulates the senses, opening new realms of possibility that may challenge or even overturn presuppositions. As in the other arts, fashion has found shock to be a powerful force to arouse attention and inspire change. At its most provocative, shocking fashion can scandalize the press and the public, while at its most intelligent, it can redefine the essential purpose and worth of a garment, generating a substantial change in what

Models walk the runway at the Maison Martin Margiela fashion show during Paris Fashion Week, 2010

Gerbert De Montreuil, "Dance at King Gascony's Court," from *The Romance of the Violet*, 15th century, France

we wear and why we wear it. Design that is both provocative and intelligent is rare, but it bears witness to shock as a compelling muse.

Some of the most shocking garments in fashion history seem to have been designed in cross-purpose to their intended function. Consider the *poulaine*, a supple slipper believed to have been introduced into the English court of King Richard II by his first wife, Anne of Bohemia (1366–1394). This simple shoe made of fabric or soft leather featured a pointed toe. Other courtiers rapidly adopted the style, and within a century the proportions became so exaggerated that the front of the shoe

had to be stiffened with a support of carved wood or whalebone so as not to trip the wearer. One version—worn exclusively by men—featured a chain attached to the toe tip at one end and anchored to a band around the knee at the other. Although by definition shoes were meant to protect the feet, the luxury materials used in crafting courtly footwear needed protection. Overshoes called pattens—clog-like wooden platforms secured beneath the sole of the slipper with straps of leather or metal over the instep—were worn outdoors to lift the expensively crafted shoe out of the dust and mud. In turn, pattens were the origin of the *chopine*, a towering

platform shoe made of wood or cork worn by aristocratic women in the courts of seventeenth-century Venice. Walking in them—one surviving pair tops out at twenty inches—required a servant's assistance. In the court of Louis XVI of France, the coiffure known as the *pouf* soared to impressive heights. Teased, piled high, and powdered with flour, these extravagant hairdos were further augmented with crowning ornaments; the notorious *coiffure à la Belle-Poule* displayed a precisely detailed scale model of a famous battleship. These extreme coiffures, as well as the wide *panniers* of courtly costume, made it difficult for the fashionably attired woman to fit in a carriage. She often had to bend her head forward to clear the roof, and she always had to ride alone.

In contrast to these courtly follies, some of the most shocking fashions of the twentieth century activated wide-ranging and enduring change. Paul Poiret introduced exotic harem pants to be worn at sophisticated soirées; within a generation women discovered that trousers could be comfortably practical as well as chic. With their short skirts, shingled bobs, and bare arms, young flappers scandalized their more decorous elders, but many mothers soon followed their daughters' daring example by raising their hemlines and cropping their hair. Through the twenties and thirties essential style lines—most notably hemlines and waistlines— were in constant flux, but the daring developments that initially triggered shock reshaped conventional attitudes. The natural body, unrestrained by a restrictive corset, no longer signified a "loose woman," and arms and legs no longer had to be concealed. As fashion became more egalitarian, it also became more fun. A scandalous style made the news, but it also generated sales. No one in a consumer society wanted to look out of date. And, through Elsa Schiaparelli's design philosophy, shock

Le Négligé Galant Orné de la Coiffure à la Belle Poule

Above: *Le Négligé galant orné d'une coiffure à la Belle-Poule*, **second half of the 18th century, France**

Left: Milanese *chopines* (16th century) in an exhibition at the Bata Shoe Museum in Toronto, 2009

became an essential component of chic. Her witty use of absurdity—a shoe for a hat, clasped hands as a buckle—was as delightful as it was disconcerting. Even the word inspired her; she chose the name "Shocking" for her favorite shade of pink, her first perfume, and even as the title of her memoir.

In the sixties, a series of shocks transformed the fashion world. Skirts rose to above the knee, and then to the mid and upper thigh, until micro-miniskirts marked the shortest women's hemlines in history. Youth trumped sophistication, and a new approach to hair and makeup redefined beauty. Even the industry changed as retail boutiques eclipsed the influential dominance of haute couture. Shock fueled fresh ideas and connoted a new spirit of freedom, and, more than ever, it became a force in fashion. One of the most startling ideas was launched by Austrian-born, California-based designer Rudi Gernreich (1922–1985). He built his reputation in the fifties with innovative knitwear designs for various American manufacturers and department stores. He established a company in his own name in 1960, but he became a household name in 1964 when he put his favorite model, Peggy Moffitt, in a monokini for a fashion shoot. The topless bathing suit—high-waisted knit briefs anchored by two thin straps—broke the previously inviolate rule that a woman always covered her breasts. Gernreich shrugged off the horrified reaction in the popular press, explaining "It was already done at private pools …. I made it official." And while the monokini did not revolutionize swimwear, Gernreich's audacity led women to question whether or not they needed a bra. Moffitt had stopped wearing hers, telling the designer, "I'm doing your clothes a disservice by wearing a bra. They look so much better without one." In the same year that she modeled the monokini, she appeared braless on a New York runway, and soon other models did the same. In 1965 Gernreich created a "no-bra bra" made of stocking-weight nylon that offered a woman the feeling of wearing a bra but next to no support. Two years later he designed a wool minidress with a high collar and long, cuffed sleeves, as well as a revealing panel of transparent chiffon across the breasts. Yves Saint Laurent responded in 1968, pairing a shorts version of his tuxedo with his first see-through blouse. Both styles were meant to be worn without a bra.

While Gernreich's shocking designs gave women the option of shedding their bras, an unorthodox combination of underwear and outerwear inspired Jean Paul Gautier (b. 1952) to revive and redefine an obsolete garment. He saw the ensemble—a Chanel jacket over a lace bra—around 1978–79, worn at a

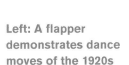

Left: A flapper demonstrates dance moves of the 1920s

Right: Portrait of silent-film actress Louise Brooks, ca. 1928

Parisian club by Frédérique Lorca, a fit model for Chanel. Gaultier enjoyed the frisson of the unexpected, thinking, "This is really new." But Lorca's exposed bra also set off a flood of memories. As a boy, Gaultier cherished the time that he spent with his grandmother Marie. She ran a modest, home-based spa, offering massage, facials, and womanly advice to a small female clientele. Gaultier's visits gave him a glimpse into the secret life of women, and he became so fascinated by their lingerie that he constructed a pair of newsprint breasts and attached them to his toy bear. Two decades later, in 1977, he made his first bustier and studded it with nails. But now, working with a traditional corsetmaker and Lorca as his fit model, Gaultier began to experiment with all the elements of corsetry: boning, laces, and support

stretch fabrics in the traditional palette of white, black, blush, and salmon pink. His first collection based on the corset debuted in 1983 with long and short dresses, as well as jumpsuits; what once was hidden was now revealed in a provocative and shocking display.

Gaultier had no interest in what he called the "orthopedic function" of the corset. He also believed that by flaunting a garment once referred to as unmentionable, he mirrored the spirit of contemporary women who were "strong and free enough to play with the rules." Madonna clearly agreed; she wore a white corset dress to the premier of her film *Desperately Seeking Susan* (1985). And in October 1989, in the early stages of conceiving her groundbreaking *Blonde Ambition* tour, she hired Gaultier to design the costumes. He drew upon

Above: Models wearing monokinis, France, 1968

Right: Danielle Sauvajeon wearing a Yves Saint Laurent design in the Paris Spring collection showing, 1968

Gaultier used the traditional features of corsetry to create an unmistakable image of sexuality and strength.

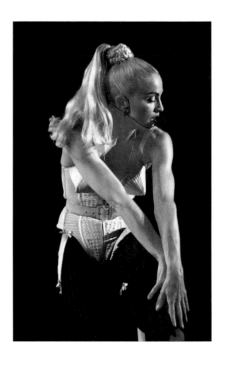

Above: Madonna arrives for the premiere of her film *In Bed with Madonna* (*Truth or Dare* in North America, directed by Alek Keshishian), Cannes Film Festival, 1991

Right: Madonna performing on stage, dressed in Gaultier's designs, in the *Blonde Ambition World Tour*, 1990

his ongoing fascination with corsetry to create an unmistakable image of sexuality and strength. Rather than contain her body, Gaultier used the traditional features of corsetry—laces, boning, and suspenders—to showcase Madonna's lithe curves. He pushed his already iconic form of the conical breast cup to the limit. And he used it everywhere: on Madonna's corsets, bursting through slits in her jackets, and even strapped to her male dancers' chests. Gaultier's designs perfectly matched the seductive and dynamic power of Madonna's performance. But Madonna did not inspire Gaultier: he had already embraced the corset as a signature design. Rather, Gaultier saw Madonna as a kindred spirit. She wore his garments with such natural force that she came to personify his muse.

Madonna enjoyed the shock waves set off by Gaultier's designs. When her documentary film *Truth or Dare* (1991) premiered at the Cannes Film Festival, she dressed in a Gaultier conical-cupped bra and girdle-styled briefs in the palest pink with a rose-colored, pink-lined cloak. She donned the ensemble in tribute to Gaultier, whose designs were "such a big part of the tour." But she also "wanted to make a splash at the top of the stairs," and she did, "in Gaultier again, in my underwear!" For the public, Gaultier's corset designs fused with Madonna's audacious celebration of female sexuality. The combination inspired a young, Michigan-born woman named Heather Renée Sweet to comb thrift shops and flea markets for old-fashioned bras and other forms of 1950s vintage lingerie. In 1993, she began to dance burlesque under the name Dita Von Teese. Von Teese acknowledges Gaultier's corset-based aesthetic and Madonna's *Blonde Ambition* tour as the sparks that ignited her imagination: "My entire burlesque career is based on my desire to wear these kinds of garments and show them off in public." She, too, has forged a special relationship with Gaultier. He invited her to walk the runway in 2007, and for the culmination of his

Marc Jacobs arrives at the Metropolitan Museum of Art Costume Institute Gala, New York City, 2012

"Parisiennes" collection (Haute Couture, Fall/Winter 2010–11) she graced the catwalk in Moins que zéro, a clinging black dress that she provocatively removed to reveal a black, strapped corset with a thong and suspenders.

In the fashion world, with its constant quest for the new, sometimes a shock is simply a shock. In May 2012, Marc Jacobs appeared at the Metropolitan Museum of Art Gala celebrating the opening of the exhibition *Schiaparelli and Prada: Impossible Conversations* in a black lace Comme des Garçons tunic worn over white boxer shorts. When asked "Who are you wearing?," he slyly replied "Brooks Brothers, I think," but he also admitted that the ensemble was a bit of a stunt: "I just didn't want to wear a tuxedo and be boring." Jacob's attire got him some attention and momentarily broke the monotony of the male dress

code; that seemed to be its purpose and nothing more. The true value of shock is far more elusive and unpredictable. To generate lasting change, a shock must engage and interrogate long-held expectations, as well as pose viable alternatives. As for the shirts in the Maison Martin Margiela 2011 collection: while no one has emulated their two-dimensional contours, the garments ignited a conversation. As a catalyst in fashion, shock has its role; but it is a difficult muse. And, according to Martin Margiela, few designers have understood this as well as Gaultier. Working as his assistant from 1984 to 1987, Margiela discovered in him "a designer who twisted things as much as he invented them." Gaultier's "freedom and daring … was very provocative, if not downright shocking for many people, and that was all for the good."

History and eritage

Some designers
discover that
history and
heritage are as
essential to their
expressive identity
as language.

When the Spanish Civil War erupted, Cristóbal Balenciaga left his homeland, and by 1937 he had opened a new salon in Paris. As the leading couturier in Spain, Balenciaga had been at the height of his career. He oversaw three dressmaking establishments and his clientele included the aristocracy and members of the Spanish royal family. He left much behind, but what he carried with him proved even more valuable. Balenciaga was a master of the craft as well as of the art of fashion; few contemporary designers could match his skill in cutting, tailoring, or manipulating fabric. He possessed an unerring sense of line and proportion, and his hallmark style featured an unparalleled balance of simplicity and splendor. But even more than his skills and his exquisite taste, Balenciaga carried with him a sense of heritage. He deeply identified with the art and culture of Spain. It informed every element of his design: color, ornament, and silhouette. And while he became one of the foremost, and most influential, Parisian couturiers of his generation, the essence of his aesthetic remained profoundly and passionately Spanish.

The influence of history and heritage on fashion varies from designer to designer. For some, history offers a lexicon of ideas to be mined for a contributing motif or an inspiring theme for an individual collection. But for others the connection with history and heritage permeates their sensibilities, and it is as deep-seated and essential to their identity as language. Some, like Balenciaga, carry their heritage to a new environment, while others remain in their homeland and embrace their national legacy as an essential component of their art. The results of this type of keen and sincere engagement with one's own history and heritage is always more than just a recycling of national dress or a reinterpretation of historical style. It is a fusing of experience and expression in which a sense of place converges with a sense of style in a uniquely personal creation. History and heritage can be powerful influences, especially when viewed through the lens of memory. And it is well worth recalling that Mnemosyne, the goddess of memory, was the mother of the Muses.

Cristóbal Balenciaga (1895–1972) spent his boyhood in Getaria, a Basque fishing village on Spain's northern coast

Cristóbal Balenciaga, France, 1927

Left: An evening dress designed by Cristóbal Balenciaga in white cotton pique cut away to show a full skirt of black silk flounces, 1951

Above left: Diego Velázquez, *The Lady with a Fan*, ca. 1640, Wallace Collection, London

Above right: Diego Velázquez (workshop), *Portrait of Infanta Margarita Theresa at Age 8*, 1659, Kunsthistorisches Museum, Vienna

where most young men sought their vocations on the sea or in the church. But when Balenciaga's father—a one-time sailor who served as village mayor—died in 1906, his mother relied upon her sewing skills to support the family. Her work sparked her son's interest, and Balenciaga's talent was revealed when, at the age of fourteen, he asked his mother's most prestigious client, the Marquesa de Casa Torres, if he could make a copy of one of her Parisian suits. His excellent replica astonished both his mother and her client; they arranged for Balenciaga to move to the elegant resort town of San Sebastián, where the Marquesa had a residence, to be trained in tailoring. By the age of nineteen, he opened a salon in San Sebastián under the name Eisa, a diminutive of his mother's name Martina Eizaguirre. Over the next decade, he enjoyed such success that he opened two more salons, one in Barcelona and the other in Madrid.

By the time Balenciaga relocated to Paris he had earned an international reputation for impeccably crafted garments made for a privileged clientele. And his debut Parisian collection, launched in the winter of 1937, did not disappoint the critics. The collection featured a series of superbly conceived black dresses, relieved only by a twist of pearls at the neckline. As subtle as they were chic, these dresses displayed Balenciaga's confidence; black fabric exposed any error in cut or fit. Balenciaga knew that his models were flawless. But, the reporter for *Harper's Bazaar* saw something just as significant in his choice of a black so rich and deep that "it hits you like a blow." This was "Thick Spanish black, almost velvety, a night without stars." In 1939, the extraordinary silhouettes of his new evening gowns caused a similar stir, and this time the Spanish connection was explicit. Nearly three centuries earlier, Diego Velázquez created a series

Balenciaga transformed traditional silhouettes and materials into sophisticated designs that always felt fresh and contemporary.

of portraits of the Infanta Margarita Theresa (1651–1673), daughter of King Philip IV of Spain. Inventing upon the silhouette and embellishments of the infanta's sumptuous garments through subtle revision and reference, Balenciaga evoked the splendor of the era. His trim, triangular bodices and wide, stiffened skirts looked strikingly new, a stunning contrast to the clinging, body-conscious line of the day. Balenciaga executed the distinctive line and proportions with such mastery that he transformed the Baroque silhouette into a thoroughly modern expression, as seen in one of the most severe models of the "Infanta" collection: a magnificent evening coat of scarlet satin opening over a layered black lace skirt.

The Infanta gowns had a specific source, but in the years that followed Balenciaga's creations revealed a consistent Spanish sensibility, expressed through color, form, and material. He had grown up in Spain, surrounded by his nation's works of art, cultural traditions, and regional dress, and they were as central to his identity as the Spanish language. Over the years he returned to basic forms derived from traditional dress—bolero jackets and mantillas, layers of flounces and lace—and through his innovative cuts and precise tailoring, he refined these forms into exquisite and sophisticated garments that always felt fresh, new, and contemporary. His

Right: A model wearing a dress and coat by Balenciaga during rehearsals for an appearance on the television show *Fashions From Paris*, 1955

Right page: A model walks the runway wearing the Alexander McQueen Fall/Winter 2008–09 collection during Paris Fashion Week, 2008

selection of colors was particularly telling. Rather than responding to a season's favorite hue, Balenciaga continually returned to the color palette of his homeland. As noted at his debut Paris collection, he favored black, a color associated with the Spanish court since the late Middle Ages. It symbolized aristocratic virtue, but there was also a material significance. Until the late seventeenth century it was difficult to dye cloth a deep black; pigments used for black dye did not dissolve well in water. To attain a true, even tone, the fabric had to be immersed repeatedly, and only the very wealthy could afford it. Black, therefore, became the color of privilege, worn by Spanish courtiers, and the pearls and starched white ruffs of

court costume, so well documented in official portraiture, further emphasized the richness of the exclusive hue. Balenciaga recognized and mastered the power of black, but he also understood the importance of contrast. In addition to bold black and white combinations, he used other colors associated with Spanish traditions: the golden yellow and deep purple of liturgical garments, the magnificent reds of the bullring, and carnation pink, paired in the traditional mode with black Chantilly lace.

The fashion press took notice of Balenciaga's aesthetic heritage. In 1948, *Harper's Bazaar* observed that his collections always resonated with "an echo of his native land" through his use of "brilliant colors, beads, paillettes,

pompoms, and the little jacket of the matador." But Balenciaga's designs never descended into cliché or masquerade. A trio of three strapless evening gowns, from his 1951 winter collection, illustrate his seamless transformation of the elements of his heritage into innovative contemporary design. His signature use of black creates austere, body-conscious silhouettes that are varied by treatments at the hem. Two dresses feature a raised hemline, recalling the *bata de cola*, the flamenco dance dress with an extended train. A skilled dancer kicked the train to flip it as an embellishment of her fluid line, but Balenciaga derives his fluidity from a perfectly balanced underskirt and overskirt, using white tulle for one dress and carnation pink flounces for the other.

Although raised in England, McQueen felt the powerful pull of his Scottish ancestry.

The third dress has a narrow hem, but he created a contrast with a voluminous swath of scarlet. Fashion historians have often described Balenciaga's handling of cloth as sculptural, but Hamish Bowles notes the "painterly treatment" of his graceful stoles; the accent they provide has the beauty and bravura of a Spanish master's brushstroke.

Throughout the fifties, Balenciaga experimented with innovative shapes: dolman sleeves, sacque dresses, hoods, capes, and tunics. His contemporaries admired his matchless skill at cutting and shaping fabric; Dior and Chanel both remarked that his mastery of construction and his unyielding standards made him the ultimate couturier. Givenchy regretted that he did not receive his training in Balenciaga's atelier. Balenciaga regarded the perfection of craft essential to design, and he always referred to his work as his métier rather than his art. Less tangible but just as essential was the role of memory. Through his designs, Balenciaga shared fleeting recollections of his homeland: the black-clad courtier, the robed saint, the fiery dancer, and the parish priest in his caped cassock. In 1968, unwilling to compromise his standards to meet the rising demands of the ready-to-wear market, Balenciaga closed his Parisian maison and retired to Spain.

The call of a distant homeland can be a powerful force, whether a designer leaves, as Balenciaga did, at midlife with fully formed sensibilities or as a child with a more fragile but none-the-less resonant visual memory. Isabel Toledo

(b. 1960) was just eight years old when her family moved from Camajuaní, Cuba to West New York, New Jersey. In her first collection for Henri Bendel (1985) she lined plain denim jackets and coats with a colorful patchwork of silk satin. It was only later that she recognized her inspiration: a memory of houses in Camajuaní: "with their stark, stucco exteriors and the bright surprise of colored painted tiles decorating the inner rooms."

And the sense of heritage can be as significant as actual experience. Although raised in England, Alexander McQueen (1961–2010) felt the strong pull of his Scottish heritage. His mother, an ardent amateur genealogist, instilled in him a deep respect for his ancestry as well as a passionate interest in Scotland's history. McQueen regarded the connection as elemental to his vision as a designer, and that connection was never more evident than in the

two collections inspired by Scottish history: "Highland Rape" (Fall/Winter 1995–96) and "Widows of Culloden" (Fall/Winter 2006–07). The raw, agonized aesthetic of "Highland Rape" directly referenced Scotland's heroic yet doomed struggle to resist British domination. The ethereal beauty of "Widows of Culloden" offered an elegy to the profundity of cultural loss. The tartans that he used—for the first time in "Highland Rape"—presented potent

symbols of heritage, but McQueen's extraordinary handling of the traditional material gave it a new and poignant meaning. To McQueen, his Scottish heritage was "everything"; but he also embraced his identity as a Londoner: "London's where I was brought up. It's where my heart is and where I get inspiration." Vivienne Westwood (b. 1941) sees her own embrace of history in the early eighties as crucial to her development as a designer. Her most "English" collections—"Harris Tweed" (Fall/Winter 1987–88) and "Anglomania" (1993–94)—built upon traditional British tailoring and textiles: the sturdy woolens of the Western Scottish Isles, the fine woolens of Savile Row, Tattershall checks, clan tartans, hunter's "pinks." The is nothing political or nationalistic in Westwood's choice; rather it's a matter of her understanding her identity: "I'm not trying to be English—you can't avoid it, it's what you've absorbed."

In 1968, when Balenciaga closed his house without an heir, he left an extraordinary heritage: an archive of iconic garments. The business was purchased and revived by Jacques Bogart in 1986, but it was not until the appointment of Nicolas Ghesquière (b. 1971) to the position of creative director in 1997 that the archive resurfaced as significant. In his first collection for the house (Fall/Winter 1997–98) Ghesquière evoked the master's aesthetic: the extravagant yet controlled silhouette, a palette ranging from subtle pearl gray to stunning scarlet, a vocabulary of such forms as hoods and tunics that recalled traditional and timeless garments. But the designs were neither a tribute nor a revival; they were strictly Ghesquière's own. In an interview with Suzy Menkes in 2001, Ghesquière reflected upon the value of the archive, stored in a locked room in his atelier. He consults it, but does not rely upon the iconic garments for his inspiration. "My relationship with Cristóbal Balenciaga is not as a heritage but as a way of looking at his work." To adopt Balenciaga's heritage as his own would be an affectation; he was raised in France by a French mother and a Belgian father. Throughout his time as creative director at Balenciaga—he was replaced by Alexander Wang in late 2012—Ghesquière's disciplined research and high standards paid respect to the house's history. But to honor Balenciaga's memory, he wisely followed his own muse.

—

Westwood's aesthetic is not patriotic: "I'm not trying to be English—you can't avoid it, it's what you've absorbed."

—

Naomi Campbell modeling a dress by Vivienne Westwood, 1994

To honor Balenciaga's memory, Ghesquière wisely recognized the need to follow his own muse.

Models in designs by Nicolas Ghesquière for Balenciaga, Fall/Winter Collection 1997–98, Paris, 1997

The American Muse

The spirit of American style—confident and casual—intrigues designers no matter their origins.

On the bitterly cold morning of January 20, 1961, John Fitzgerald Kennedy set off with his wife Jacqueline to the Capitol Building in Washington, D.C., where he was to be sworn in as the thirty-fifth president of the United States of America. At forty-three years old, Kennedy was the youngest elected president in the nation's history. Tall and energetic, with a thick mane of auburn hair, Kennedy's appearance made a striking contrast to that of his grandfatherly predecessor Dwight D. Eisenhower. "Jackie," youthful and stylish, also caught the public's eye. All the first ladies of recent history—Eleanor Roosevelt, Bess Truman, Mamie Eisenhower—had been middle-aged and matronly. But Jackie was just thirty-one, and dressed that morning in a pale wool

coat, fur-trimmed boots, and a pillbox hat, she clearly embodied a new image for American women.

Just six months earlier, Jackie had a problem with clothes. On July 13, *Women's Wear Daily* published a front-page exposé charging that she regularly spent a fortune on Parisian couture. Although the article was mostly conjecture—Jackie countered that she could not possibly have spent $30,000 in a single year "unless I wore sable underwear"—it raised serious questions within the leadership of the International Ladies' Garment Worker's Union, who had given strong support to Kennedy's campaign. Julius Hochman, director of the Union Label Department, suggested to Eleanor Lambert, a publicist working with Jackie's staff, that Jackie needed to change her image. And Jackie took

Above: President John F. Kennedy and his wife Jacqueline on the morning of his inauguration, Washington D.C., January 20, 1961

Right: Jacqueline Bouvier, photographed by Richard Rutledge, 1951

**When she became
first lady Jackie
was just thirty-one,
and she embodied
a new image for
American women.**

Left: Jacqueline Kennedy
dances with Oleg Cassini
at the Belmont Ball, Long
Island, 1954

Following double page:
Pat Nixon, Mamie
Eisenhower, Lady Bird
Johnson, and Jacqueline
Kennedy (left to right)
listening to John F.
Kennedy's inauguration
speech, Washington,
D.C., January 20, 1961

action, writing a long letter to Diana
Vreeland, the esteemed editor of
Harper's Bazaar, asking for her guidance:
"I must buy American clothes and have
it known where I buy them." By autumn,
when the campaign was in full swing,
Jackie captivated the press as well as
the public with her all-American style.

Jackie was hardly the only American
woman to have favored French fashion.
During the late nineteenth century,
affluent women ordered their wardrobes
from such Parisian couture houses as
Worth, Doucet, and Paquin. By the first
decades of the twentieth century, French
designers cultivated a broader American
market by mounting tours of their latest
collections and offering their designs
through exclusive license to select
dressmakers and department stores.
It was through these custom shops,
particularly those affiliated with Bergdorf
Goodman and Ohrbach's in New York,
that Jacqueline Bouvier Kennedy
(1929–1994) first acquired her taste
for French fashion. She had, in fact, a
passion for everything French since her
childhood. She was French by heritage,
and her education had focused on
French studies: in language, literature,
and history. Her preferences were clear
in fashion as well. After her marriage in
1953, as the wife of a young senator,
she favored the clean, sharp styles of

the designers who offered a youthful
alternative to the sumptuous New Look:
Hubert de Givenchy and Coco Chanel.

During the early autumn months of
1960, Jackie joined her husband on
the campaign trail. The press closely
followed the photogenic couple, and
Jackie's clean-lined, bright-colored
coats and suits were as closely analyzed
as her husband's speeches. Many of
the garments had long been part of
her wardrobe, and when the press
misidentified a garment—a genuine
Givenchy as an Ohrbach's replica—
she did not correct them. But for the
inauguration events, as well as her life
in the White House, Jackie needed
American designs, and shortly after the
election, a friend of the Kennedy family,
Oleg Cassini (1913–2006), offered
his services.

The Parisian-born Cassini launched
his career in film, working for Paramount
Pictures and Twentieth-Century Fox.
In 1952, he opened his own fashion
house in New York and became known
for bringing Hollywood glamour to
American design. But he had a very
different idea in mind for Jackie. As a
costume designer, Cassini had learned
to design within a story, creating a
wardrobe to suit the scenario as well as
the character. He envisioned the young
first lady in forward-looking architectural

Prince Philip and Queen Elizabeth II with the Kennedys at Buckingham Palace, London, 1961

—

Jackie's clean-lined, bright-colored ensembles were as closely analyzed as her husband's speeches.

—

Jacqueline Kennedy is greeted by the crowd during her visit in Paris, 1961

clothes made of high-quality fabrics that needed no more embellishment than their impeccable tailoring. In his designs Cassini balanced the public demands of a "state wardrobe" and the personal taste of his client. Jackie had already demonstrated her preference for a tastefully restrained aesthetic; Cassini described her style as "minimalist *par excellence*." And when Jackie saw his sketched ideas for her inauguration ensemble, she pronounced them "absolutely right."

Cassini knew that the inauguration ceremony marked Jackie's debut as first lady, and her ensemble had to set the tone for her role in the White House. He made an unorthodox yet inspired fabric choice: heavy wool melton in a luminous shade of greige. The weight of the fabric would keep her warm for the outdoor ceremony, and its substance enriched the simplicity of his design: a single breasted, collarless coat. Embellished only with

two large fabric-covered buttons and patch pockets, the coat's immaculate lines struck just the right tone of dignified elegance. All that he added was a sable circlet tucked beneath the neckline and what would become Jackie's trademark: the large, tipped-back pillbox hat. Jackie looked radiant in the crowd, neatly groomed and warm in her pale wool coat. Cassini had rightly predicted that the other women would be "loaded down with furs like a bunch of bears," while Jackie would stand out, her youthful appearance in perfect accord with her husband's vision of a forward-looking nation.

In the inaugural ensemble, as well as the wardrobe for Jackie's role as first lady, Cassini drew on a select number of elements—body-skimming silhouettes, stand-away collars for jackets and *bateau* necklines for dresses, and three-quarter sleeves—that combined her established style with his vision of her as the "minimalist *par excellence*." And he welcomed collaboration; Cassini was always willing to adjust a contour or raise a hemline at her request. Jackie often took the initiative, sending Cassini photographs of designs that she liked— with her own ideas sketched in—as well as swatches of fabric and samples of trim. He admired her taste, respected her personal preferences, and even credited her as a partner in the creation of the designs, explaining that "my job is essentially a matter of presenting ideas for her editing."

For evening wear, Cassini combined her love of simplicity with his flair for glamour by creating sleek silhouettes in fabrics with sheen and substance in

Four ladies sporting pillbox hats model the "Jackie Look," photographed by Yale Joel, published in *Life* magazine, 1961

Above: Michelle Obama wears dresses by Maria Pinto at the Democratic National Convention in Denver, Colorado (left), and at a rally in Saint Paul, Minnesota, in 2008

Right: Flag dress by Wendelien Daan for Catherine Malandrino Fall/Winter 2001–02, 2007

pale, light-catching hues. The absence of embellishment gave his gowns a streamlined, modern look. And Jackie embraced this image. Her look was consistent, whether she wore Cassini's designs or those of her former favorites, such as the slim, frost-blue silk shantung dress, created by the New York custom firm Chez Ninon after a design by Givenchy, that she worn to a dinner at Buckingham Palace in 1961. The contrast with Queen Elizabeth's full-skirted, cerulean tulle, designed for her by Norman Hartnell, is unmistakable; although only three years younger than the queen, Jackie seems to represent a different generation.

Based on Jackie's distinctive preferences, the style lines of the "Jackie Look" had ready appeal. The essential understatement of her style made it easy to recognize and replicate, and by the spring of 1961, "Jackie Look"

ensembles dominated the fashion scene. While luxury shops and custom dressmakers featured the same fine fabrics and flawless details, affordable imitations—with color-coordinated plastic buttons and machine finishing substituting for such handcrafted features as fabric buttons, topstitched seams, and decorative bows—could be found in department stores. The informal sophistication of the look also blurred social status. It was a democratic style, and therefore essentially American. Within a few months the "Jackie Look" swept the nation; women all over the United States put on simple suits and pillbox hats, because everyone wanted to look like Jackie.

In the years after the Kennedy administration, new designers, including Geoffrey Beene, Diane von Furstenberg, Betsy Johnson, and Halston, created their own visions of the American

Left page: Barack and Michelle Obama welcome Chinese president Hu Jintao at the White House, Washington, D.C., 2011. Michelle Obama wears a dress by Sarah Burton for Alexander McQueen

Left: Michelle, Malia, Barack, and Sasha Obama sit for the official White House Christmas portrait, 2011

woman. And Jackie, nicknamed "Jackie O" by the press after her marriage to shipping magnate Aristotle Onassis, asserted her own inimitable style as a chic, practical New Yorker in a trench coat or turtleneck sweater paired with slim pants and her ever-present sunglasses.

The spirit of American style—confident and casual—intrigued designers no matter their origins. In February 2001, inspired by the "vast spaces" of the United States, as well as the film *Easy Rider* (1969), the French designer Catherine Malandrino (b. 1963) debuted her own "American Dream" collection. She invented upon such uniquely American ideas as baseball and rockabilly in fabrics ranging from cashmere and leather to denim and jersey. After the tragic events of September 11, 2001, her Flag dress of flowing silk printed with stars and stripes gained special meaning; such diverse figures as Meryl Streep, Madonna, and John Galliano adopted the dress as an emblem of support. Seven years later, Malandrino reissued the dress to celebrate the historic campaign of Illinois senator Barack Obama for the presidency of the United States.

On February 25, 2008, the magazine *Newsweek* profiled the senator's wife Michelle Robinson Obama (b. 1964), who was featured on the cover in a sleeveless lavender sheath accessorized with a simple string of pearls. Soon after, magazines and websites began to track her public appearances; fashion writers hoped to portray "Michelle O" as a twenty-first-century Jackie. But, Michelle was not a constant presence next to her husband on the campaign trail; she often remained in Chicago to care for their young daughters. And although she sometimes wore sleek, architectural ensembles created by local designer Maria Pinto, it quickly became evident that Michelle was equally comfortable in garments purchased at such popular retail chains as White House | Black Market and J. Crew. She had her own sense of style, but rather than assembling a "state wardrobe," Michelle chose her clothes solely on preference.

On the night that Obama was elected, Michelle was at his side for the outdoor celebration in a stunning red and black satin dress by Narciso Rodriguez; she added a modest black cardigan for extra warmth. Unlike Jackie, who established a signature style in collaboration with

Cassini, Michelle delights in variety. For the inaugural ceremony, she chose a matching coat and dress of lemongrass wool lace, backed with cream silk radzimir, by Isabel Toledo, who took her inspiration from the fabric itself; she wanted to create an ensemble that would be warm yet comfortable. When Toledo saw the new first lady in her design she was thrilled: as the daughter of immigrants from Cuba, working with a staff from all points of the globe, she felt that it marked a truly American moment. She described the vibrantly colored dress as "happiness made visible—for Michelle and me, for our new president, and for a nation." For the inaugural balls, Michelle chose an ivory silk chiffon, one-shouldered gown by Jason Wu. With her statuesque figure Michelle made an indelible impression; Jackie, too, had worn ivory for the inaugural ball, but Michelle's dress was neither a replica nor a tribute. Like the new first lady, it was an American original.

For her role in the White House, Michelle works with stylists rather than a specific designer, and she has continued to mix custom-made garments with ready-to-wear. Unlike Jackie's image, there is no "Michelle Look." She clearly likes figure-conscious silhouettes and bright colors, but her clothing has an authentic spirit of eclecticism rather than a consistent, calculated aesthetic. As for designers, Michelle does not play favorites, and her interest in young American talent has helped draw attention to such rising figures as Doo-Ri Chung, Byron Lars, and Carly Cushnie and Michelle Ochs (Cushnie et Ochs). Her support of American design has been so strong that she drew the ire of such esteemed figures as Diane von Furstenberg and Oscar de la Renta for wearing an Alexander McQueen gown to host a state dinner at the White House for Chinese president Hu Jintao. She had selected the red

silk organza from the 2011 Resort Line, requesting that the short sleeves be replaced with broad, asymmetrical straps. The resplendent color, printed with a free-form petal pattern in black, paid homage to her guest's homeland. Days later, in a television interview broadcast on *Good Morning America*, Michelle acknowledged the criticism of her choice of a British designer for such an important event, but dismissed it as an issue of small consequence. And then she shared what she called her "motto": "Wear what you love. That's all I can say." As an American muse, Jackie inspired women to be like her, but Michelle just wants American women to be themselves.

Bottom left: Michelle Obama wearing an ensemble by Isabel Toledo at her husband's first inauguration in Washington, D.C., 2009

Bottom right: Michele Obama wearing a navy blue silk coat by Thom Browne over a royal blue dress and cardigan by Reed Krakoff at her husband's second inauguration in Washington, D.C., 2013

Right: Barack and Michelle Obama dance at the Commander in Chief's ball for the first inaugural in Washington, D.C., 2009. Michelle Obama wears a silk chiffon gown by Jason Wu. Wu also designed her gown for the second inaugural in 2013

The Princess Brides

A broadcast from Buckingham Palace on November 16, 2010, drew worldwide attention: Prince William, second heir to the British throne, announced his engagement to Catherine Middleton. For royal watchers across the nation, the news held little surprise. The couple had known each other for years, having met nearly a decade earlier in an art history class at the University of St. Andrews in Scotland. Over that time, their attachment had shifted several times from platonic to romantic, but whether friend or girlfriend, Kate proved to be a good and constant companion, so much so that the British press nicknamed her "Waity Katie." But now, the romance of the prince and his fiancée took on the gloss of a fairy tale. Kate Middleton, as well as being beautiful, was born into a middle-class family. She embodied the fantasy of a girl from ordinary society winning the heart and hand of a handsome prince.

Kate's public identity was as alluring as her story. A tall, willowy brunette with a relaxed grace and an easy smile, Kate appeared as naturally accessible as she was beautiful. Her sense of style enhanced that perception; rather than patronizing a single, select designer, Kate played the field, shopping at popular department stores ranging from the high-end Harvey Nichols to the high-street Top Shop. In all her choices she favored simplicity, as seen in the dress she wore to announce the engagement. The subtle draping of the silk jersey dress, designed by Brazilian-born Daniella Issa Helayel, had modest lines, yet it displayed her slender figure. The color—a brilliant sapphire blue—matched the sparkling stones of her engagement ring, the same sapphire and diamond ring that William's father Prince Charles gave to his mother Diana. The Issa dress was an instant hit: within twenty-four hours every other one like it had sold out of London's stores, and replicas proved just as popular. In the months that followed, all eyes were on Kate to see what she wore. But the most tantalizing topic of the fashion world was who

Left: Prince William and his fiancée Catherine Middleton, wearing a dress by Daniella Issa Helayel, celebrate their engagement, London, 2010

Right: Franz Xaver Winterhalter, *Portrait of Queen Victoria in her Wedding Dress*, 1847, The Royal Collection, London

Left: Queen Victoria
in her wedding gown,
photographed by Roger
Fenton, 1854

Below: The newlywed
Princess Margaret,
wearing a gown by
Norman Hartnell, leaving
Westminster Abbey with
her husband, Antony
Armstrong-Jones,
London, 1960

Right: MGM designer
Helen Rose working on
Grace Kelly's wedding
dress, 1956

would design the gown for the newest princess bride?

The most significant innovation in royal bridal attire can be traced to one of the least likely figures in fashion history. In 1840, when Queen Victoria—Prince William's four-times great-grandmother— married her handsome prince, Albert of Saxe-Coburg-Gotha, she broke with the tradition of wearing her coronation robes for a royal wedding and commissioned a new, cream-ivory gown of Spitalfields silk satin, embellished with lace. The gown, with its deep neckline, puffed sleeves, and full skirts, was lovely, and it displayed the young Victoria's petite yet curvaceous figure. Widely admired and reproduced in fashion magazines, Victoria's wedding gown launched the tradition of the white wedding, and her

coronet of orange blossoms—another distinctive feature of her ensemble— proved just as popular.

A century later, in 1947, when Prince William's grandmother Elizabeth married the debonair Lieutenant Philip Mountbatten, the white wedding had became a convention, and in the wake of wartime austerity, Princess Elizabeth (she would become Queen in 1952) wore a modest gown made of ivory duchesse satin. It was created for her by Norman Hartnell (1901–1979), one of the princess's favorite designers. The gown itself was austere, with a long-sleeved, V-necked, fit-and-flare silhouette, but Hartnell embellished it with exquisite floral motifs—inspired by Renaissance master Botticelli's painting *Primavera* (1482)—embroidered

Prince of Monaco courted her, and after Kelly finished filming *High Society* (1956) and *The Swan* (1956), in which she played a princess about to be married, she retired from the cinema to marry the prince.

To create her gown, Kelly turned to Helen Rose (1904–1985), the head costume designer for Metro-Golden-Mayer. As well as dressing Kelly for the films that she made at MGM, including a wedding gown for *High Society*, Rose had designed bridal gowns for other celebrities, including two for Elizabeth Taylor: one for her actual wedding to Conrad Hilton, Jr. (1951) and one for her role in *Father of the Bride* (1950). Rose's distinctive use of lace overlay sparked a widespread trend in bridal wear, but Rose refused to discuss any aspect of the design for Kelly with the press. Rose's discretion not only added to the excitement, it guarded against unauthorized copies of the gown being sold in advance of the wedding.

At the civil ceremony on April 18, 1956, Kelly appeared in an exquisite day suit of pale beige taffeta, embroidered with pink floss and enriched with Rose's signature lace overlay. It was a perfect prelude to the gown designed for the religious ceremony at the Cathedral of Saint Nicholas in Monte Carlo on the following day. Kelly walked into the church on her father's arm in a stunningly simple dress with a striking silhouette. The contours of the fitted bodice—overlaid with rose point needle lace—and a full belle skirt of *peau de soie*, were unified with a pleated cummerbund. The floating circular silk net veil, appliquéd with tiny love birds and crowned with orange blossom, emphasized Kelly's patrician carriage. Every element of Kelly's ensemble— from the pearl-embroidered cover of her prayer book to the bows on her veil—was crafted in MGM's costume department for the role of a lifetime: the transformation of an American actress into an actual princess.

The wedding of Lady Diana Spencer (1961–1997) to Charles, Prince of Wales overshadowed every other

in silver thread, sparkling crystals, and ten thousand seed pearls. Along with jasmine, lilac, and rose blossoms, Hartnell included sheaves of wheat, a venerable symbol for fertility. Thirteen years later, Hartnell also designed the wedding dress for Elizabeth's sister, Princess Margaret, when she married photographer Antony Armstrong-Jones. The sleek style lines of the silk-organza gown, enhanced with crystal beading, reflected the emerging minimal aesthetic of 1960. The fashion press praised its forward-looking silhouette, noting how the pure simplicity of the "stunningly tailored" gown suited Margaret's slender frame and tiny stature.

Victoria, Elizabeth, and Margaret were all born into royalty, but film star Grace Kelly (1929–1982) became a

princess through marriage to a prince. Born into a good Philadelphia family and educated at convent and private schools, Kelly moved to New York in 1947 to study at the American Academy of Dramatic Arts. Within three years, she had debuted on Broadway, appeared on television, and made her first films. Her innate refinement and aristocratic beauty captivated film audiences, but by playing against type as an alcoholic's beleaguered wife in *The Country Girl* (1954), Kelly won an Academy Award. That summer, shooting *To Catch a Thief* (1955) on the French Riviera, Kelly admired the gardens that she saw in the distance; she was told that they belonged to "Prince Grimaldi," and in April 1955, while attending the Cannes Film Festival, she met him. Rainier III,

royal wedding of the century. From the announcement of their engagement on February 24, 1981, to the televised ceremony on July 29, all eyes were on Charles's young and beautiful fiancée. To make her gown, Diana chose the husband and wife team of David Emanuel (b. 1952) and Elizabeth Emanuel (b. 1953). Their romantic aesthetic captivated her; for her official engagement portrait she had worn a frilled, pale-pink blouse that they had designed. With the style lines of the blouse as their template, the Emanuels created nearly fifty different designs, allowing Diana to select her favorite. And the media obsession with the lovely princess-to-be forced the Emanuels to take extraordinary precautions in guarding their work in progress. To fool the press they tossed out scraps of fabric unrelated to the gown, knowing that reporters would rifle through the garbage for clues. On the day of the wedding, alighting from the royal glass

carriage in front of St. Paul's Cathedral, Diana shimmered in the voluminous ivory silk and taffeta gown with its hand-embroidered mother-of-pearl sequins glistening in the sun. The most spectacular feature of the gown was the twenty-five-foot train, the longest in recorded royal history. The Emanuels understood the theatricality of the moment, and designed the dress to be "every girl's fantasy, a fairytale wedding dress."

In terms of her personal history, Kate Middleton (b. 1982) was the perfect storybook bride. Nearly a decade older than Diana at the time of her engagement, however, Kate radiated the cool sophistication of a woman beginning a new stage of life with the man that she loved rather than the breathless innocence of a girl in a modern-day fairy tale. And, unlike Diana, Kate did not announce the name of the designer commissioned to create her dress. The absolute discretion typified

Left: Grace Kelly, in a gown by Helen Rose, with her father John Kelly on her wedding day, Monaco, Monte Carlo, 1956

Below: Prince Rainier of Monaco and Grace Kelly during their wedding ceremony at the Cathedral of Saint Nicholas, Monte Carlo, Monaco, 1956

Kate's poised personality, and although rumors constantly circulated, the first hint of the designer's identity came on the morning of April 28, when a slim blonde, dressed in ballet flats, cropped pants, and an enormous fur-lined trapper hat, was spotted as she slipped into Belgravia's Goring Hotel where the Middleton family was spending the night before the wedding. The following day, when Kate stepped out of a Rolls-Royce in front of Westminster Abbey, the elegant lines of her ivory and white gown confirmed all speculation: she had chosen Sarah Burton (b. 1974), creative director of Alexander McQueen.

Burton first worked as an intern for McQueen in 1996, and after completing her education at Central Saint Martins College of Art and Design in 1997, she became a member of the staff. Over her years working with McQueen, she shared his fascination with historical precedent and his commitment to impeccable execution. And, in designing Kate's bridal gown, Burton followed her own understanding of the McQueen aesthetic—"bringing contrasts together to make startling and beautiful clothes"—creating a dress as well-suited to her distinctive client as to its purpose. In fact, contrast was essential to her concept; Burton envisioned the dress as a marriage of "traditional fabrics and lacework" with "a modern structure and design," and she described working with Kate as "the experience of a lifetime."

A sleek silhouette and restrained elegance gave the gown its beauty, while Burton's subtle play of historical and cultural reference gave it meaning. The lace overlay on a structured bodice echoed Princess Grace's gown, but

Diana, Princess of Wales, in her wedding dress by David and Elizabeth Emanuel, 1981

the neckline and sleeves followed
the lines that Hartnell had designed
for Princess Margaret. The exquisite
Carrickmacross lace, a traditional Irish
technique, featured the floral emblems
of the nations of Great Britain: the
English rose, the Welsh daffodil, the
Scottish thistle, and the Irish shamrock.
The pleated skirt, with its train just shy
of nine feet, resembled an opening
flower, perfect for a spring wedding. The
language of flowers also guided Shane
Connolly's design for Kate's bouquet.
She carried white hyacinth and lily of the
valley (spring and new beginnings), ivy
(fidelity), and a sprig of myrtle (lasting
love) from a bush planted by Queen
Victoria in 1845 at Osborne Palace on
the Isle of Wight. Victoria's daughters,
and every royal bride after them, had
carried a sprig from the bush in their
bouquets. Kate's bouquet included a
spray of sweet William (gallantry); Prince
William, in his dashing Irish Guards
uniform, brought that meaning to life.

Traditions were followed with wit
as well as respect. The lace-making
techniques represented something
old; a pair of diamond earrings, given
to Kate by her parents and featuring
the acorn emblem of the recently
created Middleton coat of arms, was
something new. William's grandmother,
Queen Elizabeth, lent Kate the Halo
tiara, made by Cartier in 1935 for
Elizabeth's mother, which was something
borrowed. And, like Diana, Kate had
a little bow sewn into her hem for
something blue. Completely British in
material and meaning, the ensemble
was fresh, distinctive, and thoroughly
modern. Burton, inspired by the flair and
individuality of her client, balanced two
seemingly incompatible qualities: the
gown that she designed for the royal
wedding was as contemporary as it
was timeless.

Within hours of the televised
ceremony, replicas of the dress went
into production all over the world. The
sophisticated lines and long sleeves
immediately influenced new bridal
designs, including long-sleeved gowns
designed by Ralph Lauren for Lauren
Bush and Stella McCartney for Nancy
Shevell. The August edition of *Brides
Magazine* featured a lookalike of Kate
Middleton on the cover, and when the
long-awaited film *Twilight: Breaking
Dawn* opened in November, Bella Swan
(played by Kristen Stewart) wore a
long-sleeved, lace-embellished, button-
backed gown designed by Carolina
Herrera to marry her courtly vampire.
But, despite replicas, tributes, and new
inspirations, there was only one royal
wedding gown, and when it was put
on display at Buckingham Palace from
July to October, 2011, a record-breaking
600,000 visitors went to see it. Kate
Middleton and Queen Elizabeth visited
the exhibition together, and although her
official title is Catherine, the Duchess of
Cambridge rather than Princess Kate, in
Burton's gown she was the incarnation
of the perfect princess bride.

BIBLIOGRAPHY

General

Christopher Breward. *Fashion*. Oxford, 2003.

Christopher Breward. *The Culture of Fashion*. Manchester and New York, 1995.

Gerda Buxbaum, ed. *Icons of Fashion: The 20th Century*. Munich, 2005.

Fred David. *Fashion, Culture, Identity*. Chicago, 1992.

Amy de la Haye. *The Cutting Edge: 50 Years of British Fashion 1947–1997*. London, 1996.

Elizabeth Ewing. *History of Twentieth-Century Fashion*. New York, 1992.

Akiko Fukai, ed. *Fashion: A History from the 18th to the 20th Century; The Collection of the Kyoto Costume Institute*. 2 vols. Cologne, 2006.

Jan Glier Reeder. *High Style: Masterworks from the Brooklyn Museum Costume Collection at the Metropolitan Museum of Art*. New York, 2010.

Richard Martin and Harold Koda. *Historical Mode: Fashion and Art in the 1980s*. New York, 1989.

Françoise Mohrt. *The Givenchy Style*. Paris, 1998.

Georgina O'Hara Callan. *The Thames and Hudson Dictionary of Fashion and Fashion Designers*. 2nd edition. Updated by Cat Glover. London, 1998.

Valerie Steele, ed. *The Berg Companion to Fashion*. Oxford, 2010.

Valerie Steele. *Women of Fashion: Twentieth-century Designers*. New York, 1991.

Nancy J. Troy. *Couture Culture: A Study in Modern Art and Fashion*. Cambridge, Mass., 2003.

Linda Welters and Abby Lillethun, eds. *The Fashion Reader*. Oxford, 2011.

Simone Werle. *Fashionista: A Century of Style Icons*. Munich, 2009.

Simone Werle. *50 Fashion Designers You Should Know*. Munich, 2010.

Claire Wilcox, ed. *The Golden Age of Couture: Paris and London, 1947–57*. Exh. cat. Victoria and Albert Museum. London, 2007.

Peter Wollen. *Addressing the Century: 100 Years of Art and Fashion*. Exh. cat. Hayward Gallery. London, 1998.

FURTHER READING FOR CHAPTERS

The Classical Muse
Harold Koda. *Goddess: The Classical Mode*. Exh. cat. The Metropolitan Museum of Art. New York, 2003.

Patricia Mears. *Madame Grès: Sphinx of Fashion*. Exh. cat. Museum at the Fashion Institute of Technology, New York. New Haven and London, 2007.

The Muse in the Mirror
Amy de la Haye and Shelley Tobin. *Chanel, the Couturiere at Work*. New York, 1994.

Isabelle Fiemeyer. *Intimate Chanel*. Paris, 2011.

Diane von Furstenberg with Linda Bird Francke. *Diane: A Signature Life*. New York, 1998.

Married to the Muse
Diana De Marly. *Worth: Father of Haute Couture*. London, 1980.

Valérie Guillaume. *Jacques Fath*. Exh. cat. Musée de la mode et du costume. Paris, 1993.

Harold Koda and Andrew Bolton. *Poiret*. Exh. cat. Metropolitan Museum of Art, New York. London and New Haven, 2007.

Isabel Toledo. *Roots of Style: Weaving Together Life, Love, and Fashion*. New York, 2012.

Inspired By The Arts
Dilys E. Blum. *Shocking! The Art and Fashion of Elsa Schiaparelli*. Exh. cat. Philadelphia Museum of Art. New Haven and London, 2003.

Andrew Bolton and Harold Koda. *Schiaparelli & Prada: Impossible Conversations*. Exh. cat. The Metropolitan Museum of Art New York, 2012.

Fashion Inspires Fashion

Nigel Cawthorne. *The New Look: The Dior Revolution*. Edison, N.J., 1996.

Farid Chenoune. *Dior*. Trans. Barbara Mellor. New York, 2007.

Christian Dior Man of the Century. Granville and Versailles, 2005.

Alexandra Palmer. *Dior: A New Look, A New Enterprise, 1947–1957*. London, 2009.

Muse of the Moment

Christopher Breward, David Gilbert, and Jenny Lister, eds. *Swinging Sixties: Fashion in London and Beyond, 1955–1970*. Exh. cat. Victoria and Albert Museum. London, 2006.

Shawn Levy. *Ready, Steady, Go! The Smashing Rise and Giddy Fall of Swinging London*. New York, 2002.

Mary Quant. *Quant by Quant*. London, 1967.

The Cinematic Muse

Stella Bruzzi. *Undressing Cinema: Clothing and Identity in the Movies*. London and New York, 1997.

Elizabeth Leese. *Costume Design in the Movies*. New York, 1976.

Alice Rawsthorn. *Yves Saint Laurent: A Biography*. New York, 1996.

Yves Saint Laurent et al. *Yves Saint Laurent*. Exh. cat. The Metropolitan Museum of Art. New York, 1983.

Michael Wood. *Belle de Jour*. London, 2000.

Mannequins, Models, and the Muse

David Bailey and James Sherwood. *Models Close-Up*. New York, 1999.

Harold Koda and Kohle Yohannan. *The Model as Muse: Embodying Fashion*. Exh. cat. The Metropolitan Museum of Art. New York and London, 2009.

Peggy Moffitt and William Claxton. *The Rudi Gernreich Book*. Cologne, 1999.

Shock Value

Brigitte Felderer, ed. *Rudi Gernreich: Fashion Will Go Out of Fashion*. Exh. cat. Neue Galerie Graz am Landesmuseum Joanneum. Graz, 2000.

Harold Koda. *Extreme Beauty: The Body Transformed*. Exh. cat. The Metropolitan Museum of Art. New Haven and London, 2001.

Thierry Maxime-Loriot. *The Fashion World of Jean Paul Gaultier: From the Sidewalk to the Catwalk*. Exh. cat. Montreal Museum of Fine Arts. New York, 2011.

History, Heritage, and Memory

Andrew Bolton. *Alexander McQueen: Savage Beauty*. Exh. cat. The Metropolitan Museum of Art. New York, 2011.

Andrew Bolton. *AngloMania: Tradition and Transgression in British Fashion*. Exh. cat. The Metropolitan Museum of Art, New York. New Haven and London, 2006.

Hamish Bowles. *Balenciaga and Spain*. Exh. cat. M. H. de Young Memorial Museum, San Francisco. New York, 2011.

Lesley Ellis Miller. *Cristóbal Balenciaga, 1895–1972: The Couturiers' Couturier*. London, 2007.

Claire Wilcox. *Vivienne Westwood*. London, 2004.

The American Muse

Kate Betts. *Everyday Icon: Michelle Obama and the Power of Style*. New York, 2011.

Hamish Bowles. *Jacqueline Kennedy: The White House Years*. Exh. cat. The Metropolitan Museum of Art, New York; John F. Kennedy Library and Museum. Boston, 2001.

Oleg Cassini. *A Thousand Days of Magic: Dressing Jacqueline Kennedy for the White House*. New York, 1995.

The Princess Brides

Edwina Ehrman. *The Wedding Dress*. London, 2011.

David Emanuel and Elizabeth Emanuel. *A Dress for Diana*. New York, 2006.

H. Kristina Haugland. *Grace Kelly: Icon of Style to the Royal Bride*. Philadelphia and New Haven, 2006.

Andrew Morton. *William and Catherine: A Royal Wedding*. New York, 2011.

CHAPTER OPENERS

PICTURE CREDITS

ACKNOWLEDGMENTS

My gratitude—first and foremost—goes to Claudia
Stäuble of Prestel for encouraging me to explore
this topic and for her perfect guidance at every
stage of my endeavors. Thanks as well to copy-
editor Jonathan Fox, to designer Joana Niemeyer
of April, London, and to editorial assistant Dorothea
Bethke for bringing the book into being. I am
grateful to have had such able research assistants
as Ashley L. Homitz, Michaela Anne Hansen, and
especially Kristan M. Hanson. I also thank Richard
L. Gringhuis, Laura J. Hensley, Jeanne Steen, and
Patricia Wieber for listening to ideas and sharing
their views. Most of all I thank Michal Raz-Russo,
my friend in all things fashion. Our consideration of
the fashion muse in a blog post for *Britannica Blogs*
lit the spark for this project, and, in appreciation,
I dedicate this book to her.

Debra N. Mancoff

Debra N. Mancoff is a Chicago-based writer
whose books include *Flora Symbolica* (2012),
Fashion in Impressionist Paris (2012), *Danger!
Women Artists At Work* (2012), *The Garden in
Art* (2011), and *50 American Artists You Should
Know* (2010). She is a scholar-in-residence
at the Newberry Library and a contributor to
Britannica Blogs.

IMPRINT

Front cover: Audrey Hepburn posing for a LIFE Magazine cover image. Italy, La Vigna, 1955.
© Philippe Halsman/Magnum Photos

Back cover (top, from left to right): Jacqueline Kennedy, 1961, see p. 160; Karl Lagerfeld and
Stella Tennant, 2003, see p. 121; Mary Quant, 1967, see p. 86; (bottom, from left to right):Yves
Saint Laurent, Betty Catroux (left), and Loulou de la Falaise (right), 1969, see frontispiece;
Twiggy, 1967, see p. 82; Dita Von Teese and Jean Paul Gaultier, Fall/Winter 2011-12, see
p. 124

Prestel Verlag, Munich
A member of Verlagsgruppe Random House GmbH

Prestel Verlag
Neumarkter Str. 28
81673 Munich
Tel. +49 (0)89 4136-0
Fax +49 (0)89 4136-2335
www.prestel.de

Prestel Publishing Ltd.
14-17 Wells Street
London W1T 3PD
Tel: +44 (0)20 7323-5004
Fax: +44 (0)20 7323 0271
www.prestel.com

Prestel Publishing
900 Broadway, Suite 603
New York, NY 10003
Tel. +1 (212) 995-2720
Fax +1 (212) 995-2733
www.prestel.com

A Library of Congress Control Number is available.

British Library Cataloguing-in-Publication Data: a catalogue record for this book is available
from the British Library.

The Deutsche Nationalbibliothek holds a record of this publication in the Deutsche
Nationalbibliografie; detailed bibliographical data can be found under: http://dnb.d-nb.de

Prestel books are available worldwide. Please contact your nearest bookseller or one of the
above addresses for information concerning your local distributor.

Editorial direction: Claudia Stäuble
Editorial assistance: Dorothea Bethke
Copyedited by: Jonathan Fox, Barcelona
Picture research: Mirela Proske
Production: Friederike Schirge
Design and layout: April, London
Origination: Repro Ludwig, Zell am See
Printing and binding: Neografia a.s.

Printed in Slovakia

FSC
www.fsc.org
MIX
Paper from
responsible sources
FSC® C020353

Verlagsgruppe Random House FSC® N001967
The FSC® -certified paper LuxoArtSamt has been supplied by Papyrus, Germany

ISBN 978-3-7913-4712-7

The Classical Muse

Inspired by the

he

Muse in the Mirror

rts

Mannequins,

Models,

and the

Shock

Muse

History and

Heritage

Value